EXCEL 2023

The Beginners Guide to Master Microsoft Excel from Scratch in Less than 7 Minutes a Day. Discover all the Function & Formulas with Step-by-Step Tutorials with Simple & Real-Life Examples

GEORGE J. WRIGHT

Table of Contents

Introduction

Excel is a spreadsheet-based program made by Microsoft. Formulas and functions are used to organize numbers and data in Excel.

Excel analysis. Excel is often used to organize data and look at finances. It is used by businesses of all sizes and in all of their tasks.

Some of the most common ways to use Excel are for data entry, programming, accounting, data management, financial analysis, charts and graphs, time management, task management, and financial modeling. Customer relationship management and almost everything else that needs to be organized! Excel is used a lot in the fields of finance and accounting. In reality, many businesses only use Excel spreadsheets for budgeting, making predictions, and keeping track of their finances. Excel is a tool for managing "data," but most of the time, it is used to handle financial data.

Since it is covered in math, money, and dense spreadsheet language, this part of Excel seems hard and scary to people who haven't used it before.

We use Excel in our daily lives to do things like budgeting and setting goals, students tack their syllabus, and many other things that most people do in a casual way rather than using simple software that gives concrete shapes.

In everyday life, people use Microsoft Excel to do math, analyze data, and make charts and graphs. Using calculations in columns and rows, Microsoft Excel is a must-have for putting information and data into systems and processes. This book shows you how to use Excel's intermediate and advanced formula-building tools. It also tells you why they're useful and shows you how to use them in real-world models and situations. This book does all of this by giving clear, step-by-step instructions and a lot of useful, real-world examples that are all geared toward business users.

Chapter 1: Introduction to Microsoft Excel

1.1. Understanding Microsoft Excel

Excel is a spreadsheet-based software of Microsoft Office used by a lot of people. Because the program is set up like a spreadsheet, it can be used for a different range of applications. Different types of data can be used to calculate, organize, and store data for later use. Using the Excel grid interface, you can organize almost any kind of data you can think of.

Excel's strength when it comes to organizing data is that you can change the structure and style of the data in any way you want. The most popular spreadsheet program in the world is Microsoft Excel. Spreadsheets in Microsoft Excel let you work with tables of numbers that are set up in columns and rows and can be changed using a wide range of mathematical operations and functions.

Excel lets you do basic math, use graphing tools, make macros, pivot tables, and use a wide range of other helpful tools and features. In addition to text, they may also show graphs of data, such as bar charts, histograms, and line graphs.

Microsoft Excel works on many operating systems, such as iOS, Mac OS X, Windows, Android, and Windows Phone. Spreadsheet programs like Microsoft Excel make it easier to organize and manage data. These programs use rows and columns to organize and change data. Spreadsheet rows are represented by numbers, and spreadsheet column headings are represented by letters. You can use Visual Basic for Applications (VBA) to program with Excel, and you can use Microsoft's Dynamic Data Exchange (DDE) to get data from other sources.

Why Should You Learn Excel?

Everyone works with numbers or figures in some capacity. Everybody has everyday expenses, which they pay for with the money they earn each month. Knowing one's income vs. expenses is necessary for sensible spending. When you need to examine, record, and save such numerical data, MS Excel is helpful. Let's explain this using the picture below.

Where can I find Microsoft Excel? There are numerous ways to obtain Microsoft Excel. You might get it from a computer shop that sells software as well. The component of the MS Office software package is MS Excel. In any case, you would need to buy the license key before you could download it from the Microsoft website.

1.2 Use Excel in Your Work

MS Excel is used for a wide range of jobs and projects because it is easy to use and can remove and add information without causing any trouble. Excel is a must-have for anything that involves money. Excel is appealing to many people because it lets them make new spreadsheets with its formulas. These spreadsheets can be used for anything from a basic quarterly forecast to a proper corporate annual report. Excel is often used to organize and keep track of things like project progress reports, sales leads, invoices, contact lists, and more. Lastly, Excel is a useful tool for science and statistics when working with big data sets. Microsoft says that researchers may find it easier to use Excel's graphing tools and statistical equations to do variance analysis and make sense of huge amounts of data.

Microsoft Excel is used in many different fields and is very flexible. In the following departments, you can see Microsoft Excel being used.

Computing

Microsoft Excel is helpful when you need to do calculations. It can be used for basic statistics, arithmetic, and even engineering tasks, among other things. With just a few basic formula parts, Microsoft Excel can handle calculations that need to be done many times to get to the final answer.

Make Charts and Graphs

Using charts and graphs in Microsoft Excel may help different departments understand and share statistical information.

Formatting

In addition, the spreadsheet program Excel has a way to change the way cells look. The cell formatting feature can be very helpful when you want to figure out how something works. If a certain result is found, the cells could be arranged to show it. The cell formatting feature can be very helpful when you want to figure out how something works. These are some of the uses that have been talked about so far. Microsoft Excel can be used for a wide range of tasks and activities. Today, spreadsheets are still the best way to look at a lot of data at once. Even though it's not the only tool available for managing all data jobs, it's one of the most reliable and cost-effective ways to analyze data right now.

Since it is based on what you know about how analytics work, it gives you a strong foundation for making smart data. Because of this, companies continue to talk about how important Excel is as the smartest way to get actionable insights into their functions. But this doesn't change the fact that the approach is still good.

Examples of Using Excel in Work

The Microsoft Excel application has a wide range of features and functions that make it easy to do routine work tasks. Now, let's look at how different types of customers around the world use Microsoft Excel every day.

In the Education Department

Teachers might use forms, table layouts, data tools, infographics, and algorithms to teach students in the classroom. Students can learn to analyze and solve basic mathematical, logical, and statistical problems by using Excel. Teachers can teach students by making a table and showing it in an Excel sheet. They may underline important statistics, use color to draw attention to visually appealing cells, and use bars and charts to show their points.

- ### *In the Business World*

Can a business owner, no matter how big or small, be successful and run their business without using Microsoft Excel? Can you run a successful business without using Microsoft Excel? The spreadsheet tool Microsoft Excel is used in a lot of business situations.

Commercial operations include things like setting goals, making plans, and making budgets, leading a team, managing accounts, estimating income and expenses, making sure a product has value, and managing client data, just to name a few. When Microsoft Excel is used at work, it helps make everyday official tasks more accurate, effective, and predictable. Microsoft Excel has a lot of useful functions and features, like charts, filters, conditional formatting, tables that include pivot tables and others, and financial and logical calculations.

- ### *Data Analysis and Interpretation*

When you work for an online business or website owner, it takes

a lot of time to do data analysis (blog, e-commerce, forums, etc.).

For instance, there are different ways to keep track of website traffic, sales, user reviews, marketing methods, user activity, and events. This kind of work takes a lot of time and a lot of thought, especially when things don't go as planned.

Using Microsoft Excel is good for both online business owners and their customers in many ways. Everyday tasks like filtering user data by country, filtering customer data by age, applying conditional formulas to large amounts of data, and so on, can all help you.

- ***Organizing Goals***

With the help of Microsoft Excel, you can set goals for your finances, your work, and your health. In this case, it helps to have a clear idea of what to focus on and how to stay on track.

Spreadsheets, logs, and plan papers all of which are made in Excel, are used for all of these tasks and activities to keep track of progress and make sure the project is done on time.

1.3 Download Microsoft Excel

Different ways of downloading excel

- ***Buy Microsoft Office Subscription***

Pay for an Office 365 subscription. Before downloading Microsoft Excel for long-term use, you will need to sign up for Office 365. You can instead download a free 30-day trial of Office 365 to try it out.

Go to the part of your account called "Office." Go to http://www.office.com/myaccount/ in the web browser on your computer. If you are logged in, it will take you to the page where you pay for Office.

If you aren't already signed in, when asked, enter your username and password.

The next step is to click >. On the site, there is an orange button on the left side. Install needs to be chosen. The button is on the right side of the page. The Office 365 setup file starts to download when you click it.

Depending on how your browser is set up, you may need to choose a place to save the file or confirm the download before the setup file starts to download.

Office 365 should be downloaded to your computer. Depending on the operating system of your computer, this step will be different. After double-clicking the Office setup file, you need to do the following:

When asked, say "Yes," and then wait until Office is done installing.

When asked, click Close to finish setting up the program.

Click Continue, then Agree, and then Install, type in the password for your Mac, click Install Software and then close when your Mac asks you to.

Try to find Excel. Since Microsoft Excel comes with all versions of Office 365, you can find it after the installation is done:

- From the Start menu, click on the Windows icon and type "excel" to drag up the Excel icon at the top.

- For Mac, click the search icon in Spotlight and type excel to bring up Excel at the top of the results page.

- ***Trial Method for Free***

Start by going to the page for the free trial of Office. Go to https://products.office.com/en-us/try in the web browser on your computer. If you download the free trial of Office 365, you can use Excel for free for a month.

Click on TRY ONE MONTH FOR FREE to get a free month. It's on the left side of the page.

Sign in to your Microsoft account when asked. Register your username and password to do this. If you had just logged into the Microsoft account, you may not need to do this step.

Choose next, and you'll find it near the bottom of the page.

Choose how you want to pay. Under "Pick a payment method," click debit card or credit card or one of the other options, such as PayPal, to enter your card information.

You will not be invoiced for Office 365 right away, but after your one-month trial is over, you will be billed for a year of Office 365.

Fill out the details of the payment. Fill out the payment information for the type of payment you chose. This will have your card number, billing address, the date the card expires, and other card information.

If you choose to pay with something other than a credit card, you will need to follow the on-screen instructions to enter your information.

Scroll down and click "next" to move on. At the bottom of the page is where you can find it. It will take you to the page with the big picture.

If you didn't pay with a credit card, you might have to enter your billing information and click "next" before you can move on.

It's easy to sign up. At the bottom of the page, you can find this link.

After that, you'll go to the "Office" page of your account.

Office 365 should be put on your computer.

The following things need to be done:

- ***Click Install > on the left side of the page.***
- ***Click Install on the right side of the page.***
- ***Double-click the file you downloaded to set up Office 365.***
- ***Follow the instructions that come up on the screen for setting up.***

Stop your trial before you're charged. Follow these steps if you don't want to be billed for a full year of Office 365 in a month:

- ***Scroll down and click Payment & billing under the heading "Office 365."***
- ***Click Cancel on the right side of the page.***
- ***When asked, click Cancel and confirm it.***

1.4 Extensions of Excel

Excel is a program that lets us save files in different formats. The.xlsx extension is a common Excel extension for storing basic kinds of data.

XLS was another extension that was used by default until MS Office 2007. We can store the VBA code in XLSM. It is made for macros in particular.

CSV, which stands for "Comma Separated Values," is another add-on that separates data with commas. The XLSB extension is used, among other things, to compress, store, and open files.

For example, the filename "XYZ.doc" includes a file extension of ".doc," a document file extension. There are a lot of different kinds of Excel file extensions. Let's start with the most common type of file:

XLS - Excel file extension

It is the most common extension form and the one that comes with Microsoft Office spreadsheets. Before 2007, the file extension was XLS. This extension is for a file that has different kinds of information, formats, and images. With the help of an extension, the operating system can figure out what kind of file it is and open it in Excel. From Excel 2.0 to Excel 2003, XLS is the default file format.

XLSX — Excel file extension

Spreadsheets made with Excel 2007 and later versions use this extension. At the moment, XLSX is the default file extension for an Excel file.

XML is the basis for the XSLX file format. With this method, the XSLX file format is much smaller and lighter than the XLS file format. This saves a lot of space compared to the XLS file format. It takes less time to download and upload Excel files. The only bad thing about this XSLX extension is that it doesn't work with Excel files made before 2007.

XLSM — Excel file extension

This file extension is used by spreadsheets with Excel macros that start with Excel 2007 or later. With the help of an extension, it's easy to tell if a file has a macro or not. This version protects a file from harmful macros, computer viruses, machines that have been infected, and other threats. This file extension is very reliable when it comes to macros and security.

XLSB — Excel file extension

This file extension type makes it possible to completely compress, store, and open Excel files that have a lot of data or information in them. It takes a long time to open and process an Excel file with a lot of information in it. It often crashes and sometimes gets stuck when you try to open it.

Chapter 2: Excel Interface

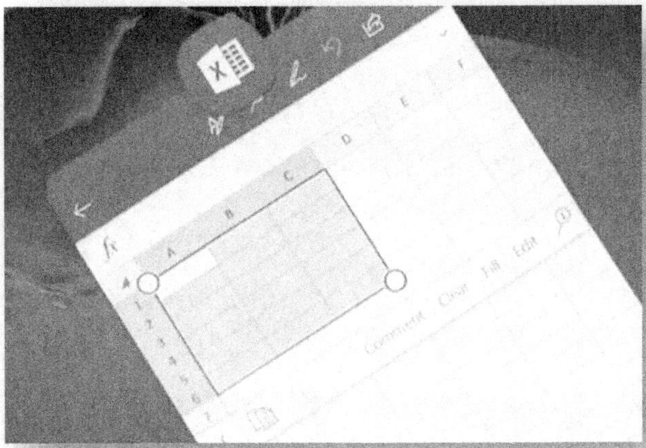

Excel 2022 is a Microsoft Office program that lets you organize, store and analyze data on a spreadsheet. If you think that only professionals use Excel to do hard tasks, you're wrong. In reality, anyone can solve problems by using all of Excel's features to their fullest.

When you first open Excel, you see the Start screen. From this menu, you can start a new workbook, choose a template, or go back to one of your old ones.

To see the MS Excel interface, find Blank Workbook on the home screen and click on it to open it. The interface of Microsoft Excel will show up in front of you.

The ribbon, which is a row of buttons across the top of the Excel window, is an important part of how the program works. The ribbon is made up of tabs, and each tab has a set of controls.

This is how you can tell where tools are located. For example, the bold button in the Type group on the Home tab is used to make the font bold for a certain range.

There are rows, columns, fields, command bars, and other things on the Microsoft Excel interface. The ribbon, which occupies most of the interface, is an example of a part that can be used for more than one thing. The Name field and the Formula Bar are two less useful but still helpful parts. This chapter will look at the interface for Microsoft Office Excel and break down each part.

2.1 Excel Workspaces

File

On the File tab, you'll find the parts of your Excel worksheet that make it work. In the INFO section, users can set a password for their workbook so that it can't be changed while they're away. Users can also check their workbooks to see if the font size is big enough for people who have trouble seeing.

You can use the NEW button to make a new worksheet that is different from the one we are working on right now. We can also use the shortcut Ctrl+N, which is pronounced "control N."

You can use the OPEN option to open and work on a worksheet you've already used. When you choose "open," a directory (folder) pops up and you can then choose the location of the file you want to open and then the file itself.

The SAVE button saves the workbook and updates it every time you save. The short-cut key is Ctrl+S.

Quick Access Toolbar

In Excel and the other MS Office suites, the Quick Access Toolbar is in the upper left corner. Save, Redo and Undo are the commands that come with the Quick Access Toolbar. The icons for Save, Repeat and Undo are already in the toolbar. Click the little down arrow at the end of the right side of the toolbar to open a box where you can add or remove icons from the toolbar.

Tell me

With Microsoft Excel's user interface, the "Tell Me" search box lets you find commands quickly and without needing to go to a ribbon tab or group. You can type the name of any command you want to use on the Sheet/Document here.

Title Bar

At the top of the Excel spreadsheet program, there is the title bar where you can see the name that is currently being used (MS-Office suites). In the middle of the title bar is the name of the book. What we called it here is what it's called in the book.

Sign in—Excel User Interface

You can buy, activate, and use Microsoft services with your free Microsoft account. The service lets you store documents and send and receive them from anywhere. You can also use this account to get to Skype, One Drive, and the Microsoft Store.

Share—User Interface

This choice is in the upper right corner, next to the button that says "Close." If you share with care, you may be able to save your work on more than one platform. Some of these platforms are One Drive, Google Cloud, E-mail, and Blogs.

Ribbon

The ribbon is the most important part of how Microsoft Excel works, and it has all the instructions you need to do the most basic tasks. The ribbon has tabs, and each tab has a lot of command groups.

- ***Home: This tab has the commands you use most often, like copying and pasting, finding and replacing, filtering, sorting, and formatting your data.***

The home tab is the default setting of Excel. It has different ribbons, such as Cut (Ctrl+X), Copy (Ctrl+C), and Paste (Ctrl+V), which can all be accessed from the clipboard. Also, the format painter lets us change the style of a whole chart, dataset, or another object with just two clicks. As the name suggests, the clipboard works like a text document (white or blackboard). Everything you copy, cut, or format creatively is temporarily stored there (as a backup) till you paste it where you want.

Because of this, you can copy and paste from one workbook to another or from one page to another, or from Excel to Word or PowerPoint and back again.

The font ribbon has tools for fonts like the name and size of the font. It lets you make your text "Bold, Italic, or Underline." You can also change the color of the font and the color of the fill. By default, the font color is set to black, but you can use Excel to change it to red or green. The color of the cell where the data is written is the same as the color of the fill.

- ***Alignment: As the name suggests, the alignment ribbon gives us options for how to line up words and numbers to the right, left, center, down, or up. If the columns are very narrow and the column title is longer than***

the column width, we can use orientation to tilt our text diagonally or vertically. There are also the "Wrap Text" and "Merge & Center" options.

On the Number ribbon, you can choose how to format both numbers and other kinds of figures. Besides the default format, general, we can also use Numbers, Text, Time, Currency, Accounting, Short and Long Dates, Fractions, Percentages, and Scientific. We also have a certain way to format numbers that need more work. It means that when you format "345" as Currency, the sign for the Naira (or any other international currency) should be in front. And when you turn 0.23 into a percentage, you get 23%. The number of digits after the decimal point can be changed in integers.

- ***Styles: This ribbon may have options that help us format our writing based on certain rules. For instance, we can set up our worksheet so that any numbers over 50 are colored in any color we want.***

On the other hand, a cell could have a green arrow to show a profit and a brown arrow to show a loss. Instead of a list of data, our dataset could be set up as a table. The Ctrl+T shortcut is on the keyboard for making a table. We can format our cells with italics, colors, headers, and other options.

- ***Cell: The cell ribbon has options like Insert, which adds a new cell between two existing ones, Delete, which gets rid of the highlighted cell or cells, and Format allowing users to adjust the column or row width or height of cells.***
- ***Editing: The Editing ribbon has quick math functions like AutoSum, which adds up all the integers in a row or column. Click Clear to get rid of all the values that have been chosen. You can sort and filter, as well as use Find (Ctrl+F) and Replace (Ctrl+H).***
- ***Commands: A command is a member of a group. You'll also be able to see a certain piece of work. For example, the Font group has instructions for italic, bold, underline, and other options.***
- ***Name Box: In an Excel worksheet, the Name Box lets you look at the reference (address) for a single cell or a range of cells, as well as give that cell or range of cells a name.***

- ***Functions to Insert: It helps get the desired result by using a certain function based on what it is given.***
- ***Formula bar: In the Formula bar, you can look at and change the formula or function that is used for any calculation in any cell on the sheet. The bar above the columns in an Excel sheet that can be resized is called the "formula bar." For better graphics, everything we type into a cell shows up above it. Before pressing Enter, it's a great way to format formulas (run).***

You can choose what kind of functions you want to do in the function box on its left. Say you want to find the lowest (MIN), average (mean), or highest (MAX) number in a set of numbers. The box for the name is on the left. It shows and tells you what cell you are in, like A1.

Row and Column Headings

The column is made up of vertical lines that are a light gray color and have the letters that are used to name each column in a spreadsheet. At the top, it has a column header (above the first row). Each row on a worksheet is marked by a group of light grey horizontal lines with a number. At the top of the page, you can see the Row Heading (left of the first column). If you don't have Column and Row Headings, you can't use Excel's autofill feature. It's one of the most important features of Excel.

Vertical/Horizontal Scrollbar

You can see any part of the worksheet by using the Vertical or Horizontal scrollbar to move up, down, right, or left.

Page View

One of the Page View Options is on the taskbar on the right side of the screen. These things are typical;

- ***Normal: This is the worksheet's default view, and it makes it easier to work.***
- ***Page layout: In Page Layout mode, the worksheet is broken up into different page sizes so that you can see how it will print.***

- ***Page Break Preview: This shows the worksheet as separate pages with content so you can see how a page looks.***

Zoom Slider/Toolbar

You can change the size of an Excel spreadsheet by using the Zoom slider, which is in the bottom right corner of the workbook.

Page Layout

With this tab, you can set up and print pages. It sets the margins, alignment, layout, and print area of the worksheet.

Formulas

On this tab, you can change the values of calculation parameters and enter function name variables. It makes the decisions about how to compute.

Data

This tab has controls for changing the data in a worksheet and connecting it to other sources of data. It has tools that let you sort, filter, and change data.

Review

This tab is mostly used to check spelling, keep track of changes, make notes and comments, share, and protect worksheets in Excel workbooks.

View

From the View tab, you can switch between worksheets, freeze panes, see Excel worksheets, and organize and control many windows.

Help

You can only use this function in Microsoft Excel 2019 and 365. This tab brings up the Help Task Pane, where you can quickly get in touch with Microsoft Support, give feedback, and watch training videos. There is an extra tab in the Excel Ribbon that can't be reached by default. This is called the developer. To get to the developer tab, click the File tab, then go to Options, click "Customized Ribbon," choose the developer option, check the box, and click OK.

2.2 Worksheets

What is an excel worksheet?

A worksheet is an array of columns and rows. When a row and a column meet, they make a cell. Cells are used to store data. A cell address is used to find out who is in each cell. The columns are named with letters, and the rows are named with numbers.

A workbook is a book with a bunch of worksheets in it. Excel starts with three cells in a workbook. You can add more sheets or get rid of some to meet your needs. By default, the sheets are called Sheet1, Sheet2, and so on.

How to create an excel worksheet

Here are the steps you need to take to make a new Excel worksheet.

When you open Microsoft Excel, you can choose from several worksheets by default, as shown below.

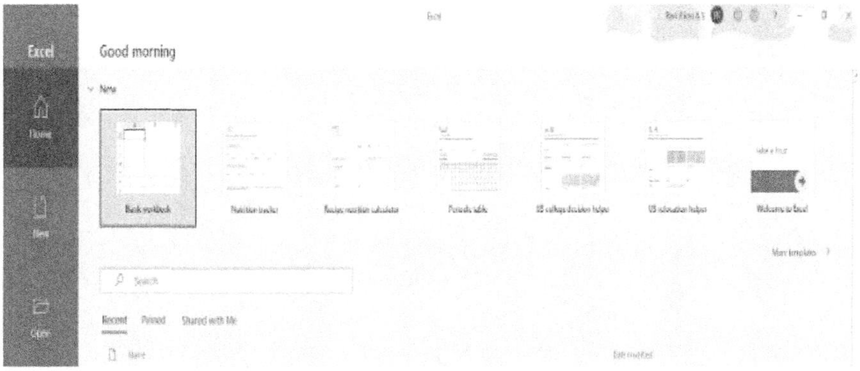

You can choose the option based on what you want to do. Make a blank worksheet for now. Here is what the blank worksheet looks like.

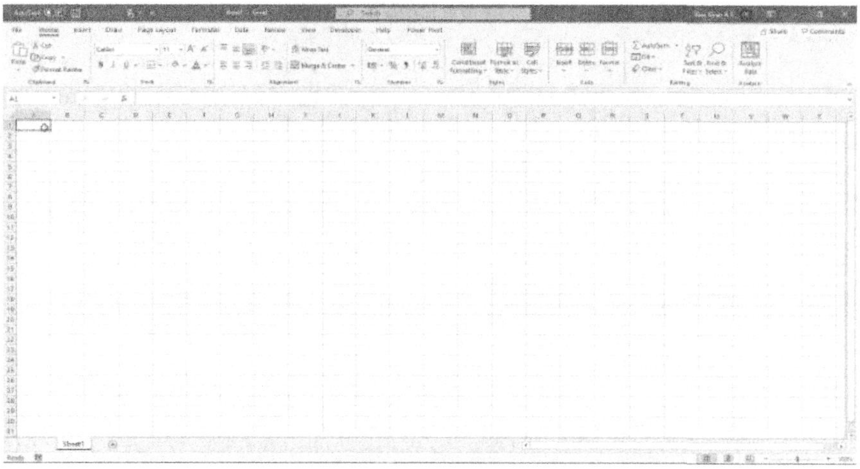

How to insert a new worksheet

There could be a time when you need to add another worksheet to the side of the one you already have. An Excel Workbook is the name for this group of Excel Worksheets. You can add a new worksheet by right-clicking on the name of the sheet in the sheet tracker tray at the bottom, as shown below.

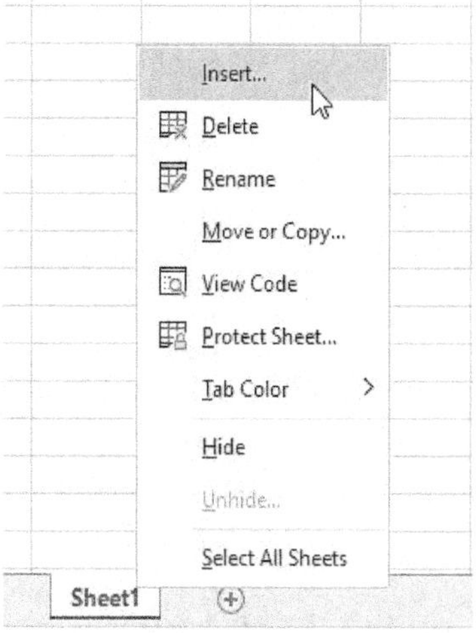

By choosing "New Worksheet" from the list of choices, you can make a new worksheet like the one shown below.

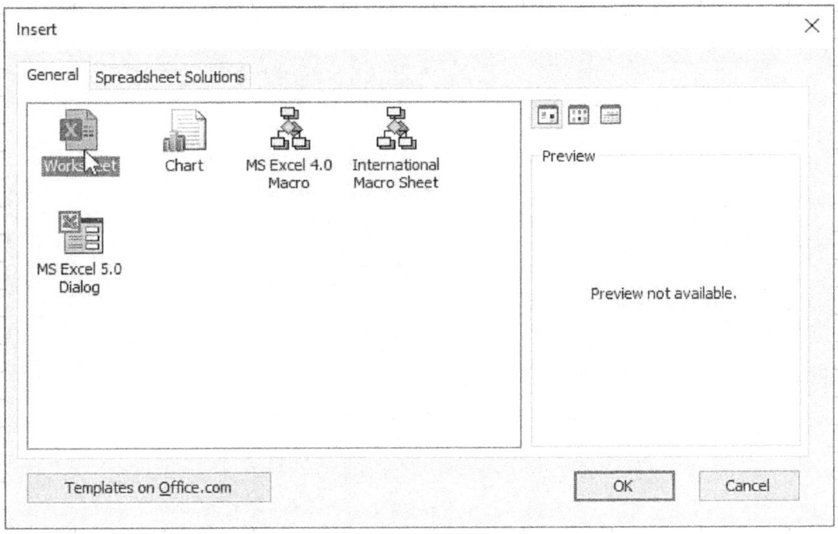

A new dialogue box will show up on the screen, where you can choose the option to add a new sheet.

How to rename an excel worksheet

You can change the name of an Excel Worksheet by right-clicking on the name of the sheet and choosing "Rename" from the menu that pops up.

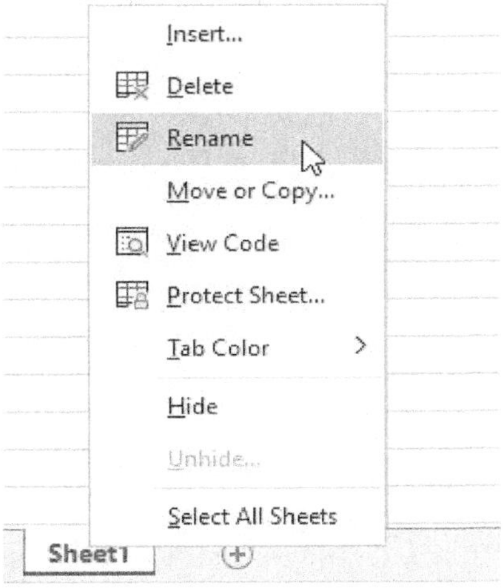

How to delete an excel worksheet

If you want to delete the Excel Worksheet, you have to right-click on the worksheet tab and choose "Delete" from the menu that pops up.

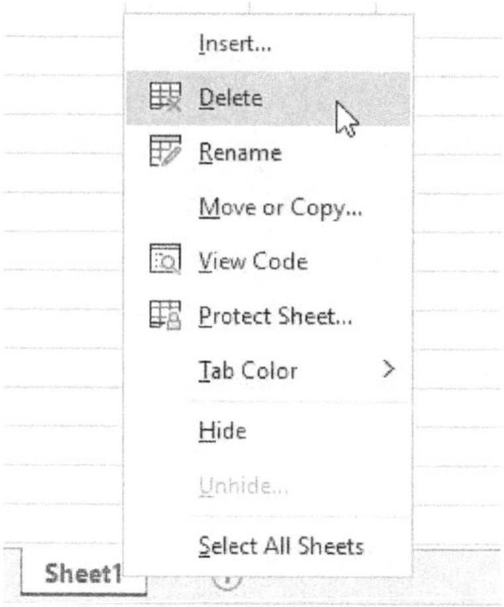

How to hide excel worksheet

Sometimes, you may need to hide a certain worksheet. You can do this by right-clicking on the name of the worksheet in the worksheet tray and choosing "Hide" from the dialogue box.

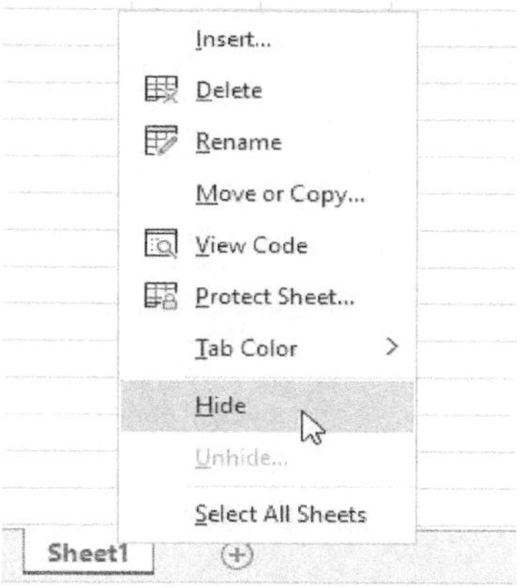

How to move or copy an excel worksheet

When you want to move or copy the Excel worksheet, right-click on the name of the sheet and choose "move" or "copy" from the dialogue box that appears.

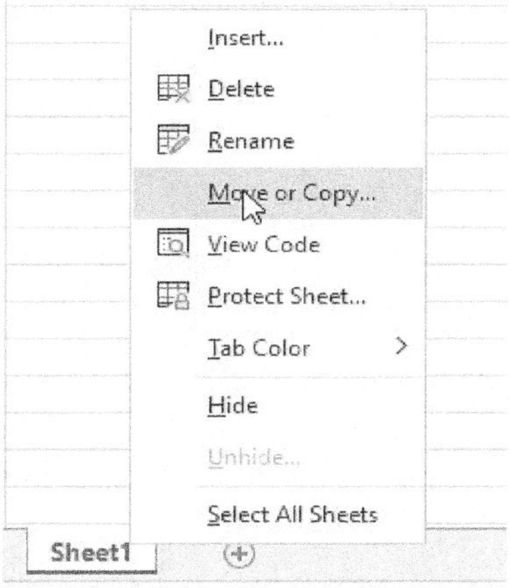

After you choose the option, a new dialogue box will appear, as shown below.

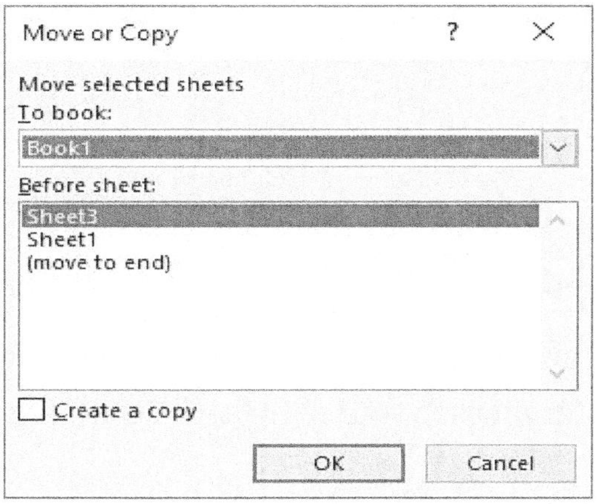

The first step is to choose the workbook in which you want to copy or move the existing worksheet. As shown below, it can be the same workbook or a different one.

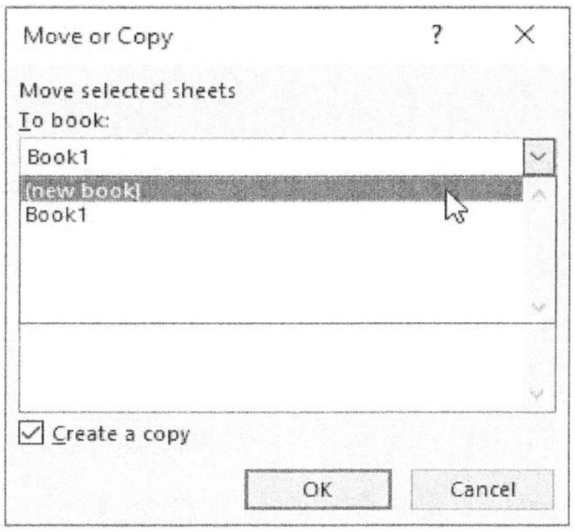

The next step is to choose whether you want to move the worksheet (cut and paste) or copy it. If you want to make a copy of the sheet, make sure to check the box shown below.

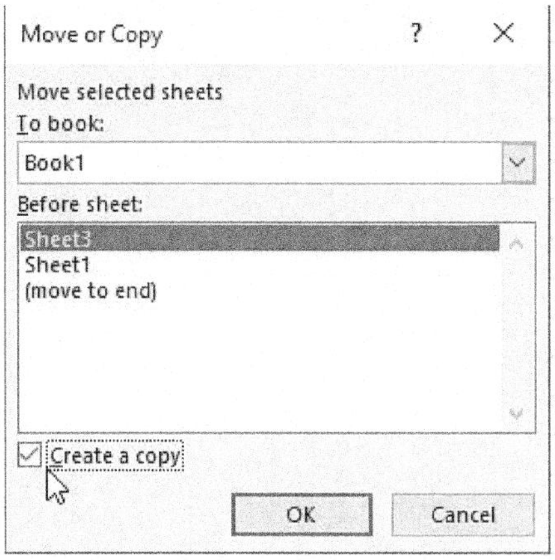

If you want to move the worksheet to a new workbook, choose "new workbook" from the first menu and leave the "make a copy" box unchecked in the last menu.

2.3 Cell Basics

Data, or "content," is placed into "cells" whenever you use Excel. Worksheets are made up of cells, the most fundamental element. To perform calculations, analyze data, and organize it in Excel, you will need to familiarize yourself with cells and the content of cells.

Understanding cells

Each worksheet contains numerous rows and columns of rectangular boxes known as "cells." The point where one row meets another is known as a cell. This is the intersection of two rows or columns.

Rows are labeled with numbers (1, 2, 3), and columns with letters (A, B, C). Based on its column and row, each cell has a unique name or cell address.

Keep in mind that the cell address is also displayed in the Name box in the upper left corner and that the column and row headers are highlighted in a cell that has been highlighted.

Furthermore, you can pick many cells simultaneously. The term "cell range" refers to a specific set of cells. In place of a single cell address, you can refer to a range of cells by specifying the beginning and ending cell addresses of the range, separated by a colon. A range of cells that starts with cell A1 and ends with cell A5 might be represented by the notation A1:A5.

How to select a cell

To enter or change the content of a cell, you must first select the cell.

- ***To select a cell, just click on it.***
- ***When you choose a cell, a border will appear around it, and the column and row labels will be highlighted in bright yellow. Once you click another cell in the worksheet, the selected cell will return to its original state.***

Cells can be selected with the keyboard's arrow keys as well.

How to select a cell range

The need to select a range of cells or a bigger group of cells arises occasionally.

- ***You can select multiple adjacent cells by clicking, holding, and dragging the mouse.***
- ***Put down the mouse to pick a range of cells. Until you deselect the cells by clicking somewhere else on the worksheet, they will remain highlighted.***

Cell content

Data entered into a spreadsheet is kept in individual "cells." Text, formatting, formulae, and functions are all valid contents for a cell.

- ***Letters, numerals, and dates are all examples of text that can be stored in a cell.***
- ***Cells can have formatting properties that alter the appearance of text, numbers, and dates. Depending on the context, a percentage might be written as 0.15 or 15%, for instance. The color of the text and backdrop in a cell is also modifiable.***
- ***Cells may also contain formulas and functions that determine the value of the cell.***

How to insert content in a cell

- ***To select a cell, just click on it.***

- ***Put some text in the chosen cell and hit the Enter key. Both the cell and the formula bar will update with the new information. A cell's content can also be entered and edited in the formula bar.***

How to clear or delete cell content

- ***You can erase content from a single cell or multiple cells by selecting them.***
- ***Click the Clear button under the Home tab's Contents section.***
- ***The data in the cell will be erased.***

Multiple cells' contents can be removed with a single press of the Delete key. To use the Backspace key to delete content from several cells, select the cells you want to delete from and then press the Enter key.

How to delete cells

Removing a cell's contents and deleting the cell itself are two very different things. If you remove an entire cell, the cells below it will move up to fill the void.

- ***Delete a cell or many cells by clicking on them.***
- ***Go to the Home tab in the Ribbon and look for the Delete command.***
- ***The lower cells will move up to cover the empty space.***

How to copy and paste cell content

Using Excel's copy-and-paste feature, you can quickly and easily transfer data across cells that have previously been typed.

- ***You can clone only one cell or several cells at once.***
- ***To copy something, either use the shortcut Ctrl+C or access the Copy command via the Home tab.***
- ***Choose the cell or cells you want to paste into. A dotted outline will appear around the duplicated cell(s).***
- ***Select Paste under the Home menu, or use the keyboard shortcut Ctrl+V.***
- ***In other words, the material will be copied and pasted into the chosen cells.***

How to cut and paste cell content

Instead of duplicating the information in a cell by using copy and paste, you can shift it around by using cut.

- ***Choose the cell or cells you want to delete.***
- ***Just utilize the mouse's right-click menu to access the Cut option. Use the shortcut key combination Ctrl+X on your keyboard, or access the command directly from the Home tab.***
- ***Choose the target cells for the paste. A new dashed border will surround the removed cells.***
- ***To use the Paste command, right-click and pick it from the menu. If you want, you can also use the shortcut key combination Ctrl+V, which will take you to the corresponding command on the Home tab.***
- ***The selected cells will have their content copied from the ones that were cut.***

How to drag and drop cells

To rearrange the contents of a cell, simply drag it to the new location and drop it there.

- ***Simply choose the cell(s) you wish to relocate.***
- ***To choose a range of cells, move the mouse pointer to the edge of the area you want to work with and wait for it to transform into a set of four arrows.***
- ***To reorder the cells, simply click and drag.***
- ***Allow the mouse to free itself. Dropping the cells there is the next step.***

2.4 Operation with Rows and Columns

Excel cells, ranges, and tables are made up of rows and columns, two distinct but interdependent Excel elements. Columns refer to the vertical sections of an Excel spreadsheet. 256 of these might be found on a single spreadsheet. Rows refer to the horizontal columns in a worksheet. You can have 1,048,576 of them, for instance.

Excel's rows and columns are like a spider web. A cell consists of a pair of contiguous rows and columns. Millions of these cells can collect and store information on a worksheet. The primary function of Excel is to facilitate the plotting and manipulation of data to facilitate insightful analysis.

How to add a new row

To insert a new row, select the header of the row beneath the one you wish to add to. The row can be selected by right-clicking anywhere on it. Select Insert from the menu options.

How to add a new column

To add a new column, select the column header to the right of the desired location. Use the right mouse button to select any cell in the highlighted column. Choose Insert on the menu.

Deleting a row or column

To erase a whole column or row, select it by clicking on its heading. You can right-click on any highlighted column or row to access its contents. Pick "Delete" from the drop-down option.

Adjusting Row height

Select an entire row by clicking on its heading. For editing the highlighted row right-click on any cell; a custom row height can be set by selecting Row Height... from the menu and entering a new value. It's worth noting that by choosing many rows at once, you can alter the row height for all of them at once.

Adjusting Column width

To choose a full column, click on its header. Use the right mouse button to select any cell in the highlighted column. Select Column Width... from the menu and set the desired width for the columns. Take note that by choosing multiple columns, you can change the column width for all of them at once.

Copying Rows and Columns

Highlight the desired rows or columns to choose them. To use the context menu, right-click on any highlighted cell. Select Copy. When you copy the selected cells to the Windows clipboard, it happens undetectably. Bear in mind that Windows only stores the most recently copied information in the clipboard.

Pasting Rows and Columns

To paste copied data, choose the column(s) or row(s) you wish to paste it into (i.e., from the Windows clipboard). Be aware that the size of the pasted data must exactly match the size of the selected area. To use the context menu, right-click on any highlighted cell. Just select Paste.

Alignment of an Entire Column or Row

When you click a column or row header, the entire column or row will be highlighted. To choose between left, center, and right justification, use the corresponding buttons on the Formatting Toolbar. You'll find these three options to the right of the standard font adjustments (italics, bold, and underline).

Chapter 3: Formulas

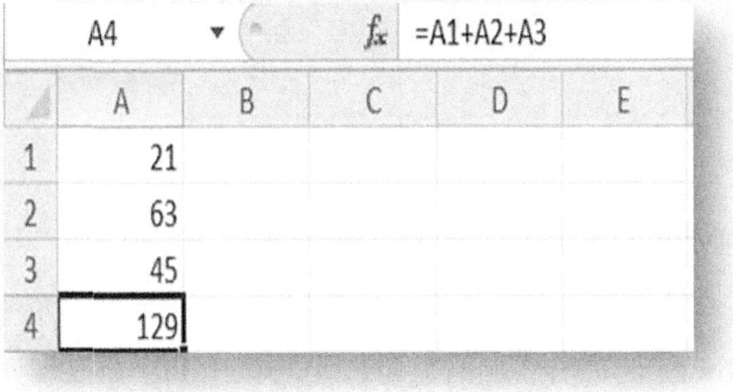

Most marketers will feel like they've hit a brick wall when they try to use MS Excel to organize and analyze spreadsheets. As you scribble long-form math on a piece of paper and redraw columns by hand, you think to yourself, "There must be an easier way to do this."

Microsoft Excel may be picky in this way. One way to look at it is as an excellent tool for analyzing marketing results and keeping track of them. On the other hand, if you don't have the right experience, it's easy for it to hurt you. Microsoft Excel, for example, will run about a dozen important formulas for you, so you don't have to look through thousands of cells on your desk.

3.1 What is an Excel Formula?

You can use formulas in Microsoft Excel to find connections between values in your worksheet's cells, do math on those values, and then return the outcome to any cell you want. Formulas like sum, ratio, subtraction, average, aggregate, and dates/times of events can be run automatically.

With Microsoft Excel formulas, you can do math and make sense of a lot of data at the same time. You can do a lot in Microsoft Excel if you know how to use a few key formulas. This can make you more productive and less likely to make mistakes with measurements. Some formulas are hard to understand, but a good one shouldn't be. Some of the most useful formulas are the ones that help you make the most of Microsoft Excel.

In Excel, a formula is an expression that works with the values in one or more cells. For instance, =A1+A2+A3 finds the sum of the values in cells A1 through A3.

3.2 Basic Math Excel Formulas

These are some basic Excel formulas that you should know if you want to work in Excel more easily.

Sum

All formulas in Microsoft Excel use the equals sign, =, along with a text tag that tells Microsoft Excel what formula to use.

In MS Excel, one of the most common ways to find the total or sum of two or more numbers in a worksheet is to use the SUM formula.

To use the SUM formula, type =SUM followed by the numbers you want to add (value 1, value 2, and so on).

The SUM function can be used to add up real numbers or the value of a certain cell in your spreadsheet.

For example, to find the SUM of 30 and 80, write the following formula in a cell: =SUM (40, 80). When you press "Enter," the cell shows the total of the two numbers, which are 120.

For example, to get the sum of B2 and B11, write the following formula in a cell: =SUM (B2, B11). When you hit "Enter," the cell will figure out the sum of the numbers in cells B2 and B11. If neither cell has any numbers, the result of the formula will be 0.

Consider the fact that you can use Microsoft Excel to find the sum of all the numbers in a list. Use the following formula in a cell of a spreadsheet to find out how many numbers are in cells B2 through B11: =TOTAL (B2:B11) (B2:B11). Instead of a comma, there is a colon in every cell.

Percentage

To use the percentage formula in Excel Spreadsheets, you need to type =A1/B1 into the cells where you want to find a percentage. To change a decimal number to a%, select that cell, go to the Home tab, and select "Percentage" from the digits' menu.

Even though Microsoft Excel does not include a "formula" for percentages, it makes it easy to convert the value of any cell to a%, so you don't have to waste any time measuring and reentering the numbers.

The option to change the value of a cell to a percentage can be found on the Home tab of Microsoft Excel. Select Conditional Formatting from the drop-down menu next to this column, and then select the cell(s) you want to change to a percent.

Then, from the drop-down menu that comes up, choose "Percentage." The meaning of each cell you have marked will be changed into a percentage. You'll find it about halfway down the page.

Remember that if you use other formulas, like the division formula (=A1/B1), to make new numbers, the results will be decimals. Before or after you use this algorithm select the cells and use the home tab to change their format to "Percentage."

Division

Type =B1/C1 into the cells you want to divide in Excel to use the division formula. In this formula, "/" is used to separate cell B1 from cell 1C. For example, if B1 is 4 and C1 is 8, =A1/B1 will return the decimal value 0.5.

Division is one of the most basic things you will do in Excel. To do this, choose an empty cell and type "=" followed by the two (or more) numbers you want to divide, separated by "/." The answer should look like this: =B2/A2.

When the Enter key is pressed, the ideal quotient will show up in the cell that is highlighted.

3.3 Other Basic Formulas

Date

The formula for DATE in MS Excel is DATE =DATE (year, month, day). This formula will give you a date based on the information in the brackets and the values in other cells. Suppose A1 is 2019, B1 is 8, and C1 is 12.=DATE(A1, B1, C1) gives you 8/12/2019.

Sometimes it can be hard to put dates in the right cells of a Microsoft Excel database. Dates are easy to format, thanks to a simple formula. There are two ways to use this formula:

Use a set of cell values to make dates. Choose an empty cell, type "=DATE," and then place the values of the cells that compose the date you want in parentheses, beginning with the year and month number, and concluding with the day. DATE= (year, month, day).

Set a date that is always today. Choose a cell that isn't being used and type =DATE(YEAR(TODAY()), MONTH(TODAY()), DAY(TODAY()) in it.

If you click "Enter," your MS Excel spreadsheet will show the most recent date.

Think that your version of Microsoft Excel is set up differently. When you use the date formula in Microsoft Excel, the date that you get back must be in the format "mm/dd/yy."

Maximum and Minimum

Determine the highest and lowest numbers in a given range with the help of the maximum and minimum (MAX and MIN) functions.

Minimum = MIN (value1, [value2]...)

Example:

The formula =MIN(C11:B2) returns the minimum value in column C and the minimum value in column B between row 11 and column C, column C2.

MAXIMUM =MAX (integer1, [integer2]...)

If you type =MAX(B2:C11), the computer will find the biggest integer in both columns B and C, starting at position B2 and continuing through row 11.

3.4 Keyboard Shortcuts

Excel has a large number of keyboard shortcuts that enable you to work faster and get more done. Instead of using the mouse to get to the toolbar, two or three keystrokes are used to do important things. Isn't that simpler and faster? Using Excel shortcuts speeds things up a lot, which cuts down on work time.

The answer to the question of whether you have to remember these shortcuts is no. But it would be helpful if you could remember at least a few of them. You will be able to recall most of the common Excel shortcuts if you use them often.

Let's now focus on the Excel shortcuts cheat sheet that you should know if you work with Microsoft Excel. In this topic, there are 50 Excel shortcuts divided into groups based on what they do. First, look at the short-cut keys for the workbook.

Workbook Shortcut Keys

Let's learn how to use a workbook in the most basic way. We will learn how to open an existing workbook, create a new workbook, and save a spreadsheet so that you don't lose any data or calculations. Then, we'll talk about how to switch between different sheets in a workbook.

Ctrl + O —Opening an existing workbook

Ctrl + N —For creating a new worksheet

Ctrl + S —Saving a workbook

Ctrl + W —Closing a workbook

Ctrl + F4 —For closing excel

Ctrl + Page Down —Moving to the next sheet

Ctrl + Page Up —Moving to the previous sheet

Alt + A —Going to the data tab

Alt + M —Going to the formula tab

Alt + W —Going to the view tab

Those are the shortcuts in Excel that you can use to move around your spreadsheet. Once the workbook has been made, the next most important step is to format the cells.

Cell Formatting Shortcut Keys

In Excel, all of the information you are working on is in a "cell." You can use shortcuts to edit a cell, align its contents, add a border to a cell, add an outline to all of the selected cells, and do many other things. Here is a sneak peek at some of the shortcuts for Excel.

F2—For editing a cell

Ctrl + C —For copying cells

Ctrl + V —For pasting cells

Ctrl + **B** —To bold

Ctrl + **I** —To italicize

Alt + **H** + **A** + **C** —For center aligning contents of the cell

Alt + **H** + **B** —For adding a border

Alt + **H** + **H** —For filling color

Ctrl + **Shift** + **&** —Adding outline to selected cells

Ctrl + **Shift** + _ —For removing outline border

Tab —Moving to the next cell

Shift + **Tab** —Moving to the previous cell

Ctrl + **Shift** + **Left Arrow** —Selecting all cells on the left

Ctrl + **Shift** + **Right arrow** —Selecting all cells on the right

In addition to the cell formatting shortcuts that have been already discussed, let's take a look at a few more advanced cell formatting shortcuts that might come in handy.

Learn how to write a note in a cell. Comments are a good way to give more information about the content of a cell. Also, learn how to find a value in the spreadsheet and change it to another value. After that, learn how to add the current time and date, turn on a filter, and add a link to a cell. Lastly, look at how to put a format on the information in a cell.

Shift + —Adding a comment to a cell

Shift + **F10** + **D** —For deleting a comment from a cell

Ctrl + **H** —To find and replace the display

Alt + **Down Arrow** —For activating the filter

Ctrl + **Shift** +**:** —For inserting current time

Ctrl +**;** —To insert date

Ctrl + **K** —Inserting a hyperlink

Ctrl + **Shift** + **%** —Applying percent format

Ctrl + **Shift** + **$** —Applying currency format

Chapter 4: Functions

Functions in Excel are predefined formulas. By giving them simple titles, they eliminate the time-consuming manual entering of formulas. =SUM, for example (B1:B3). The function totals all of the values in the B1 to B3 range.

4.1 Difference Between Function and Formula in Excel

Have you ever resorted to Excel as a flashy calculator? In that case, you could use an Excel formula. A simple formula might be something like =A1+A2 or =452*12. It's acceptable to use a formula if that's all you require. However, Excel is capable of even more.

Function and formula are often used synonymously, but they are quite different. That being said, what exactly is the distinction? A cell's value can be calculated with the help of a formula, which is an expression that refers to other cells or employs hard-coded numbers. However, functions allow you to accomplish far more than even the most basic formulas (which are sometimes all that is needed to achieve the proper answer).

A function can be defined as a formula that is already accessible in Excel. Using a function to create a computation is much quicker than doing it by hand. More than 500 unique Excel functions, including XLOOKUP, IFS, LET, and LAMBDA, are already available, with more being introduced regularly to Microsoft 365. Functions can perform sophisticated calculations that would be highly time-consuming to code by hand. To sum up a set of cells without a function, you would, for instance, type =B1+B2B3B4+B5 instead of =SUM (B1:B5). It's not a big deal to handwrite for just five cells. Now suppose you want to expand by hundreds of cells. Hundreds, maybe? As you can see, functions greatly simplify the process and are key to Excel's utility.

In Excel, a formula can be any kind of calculation, whereas a function is a specific kind of computation that has already been specified.

4.2 Basic Useful Functions

Excel can perform over 475 unique functions. When you're just starting in the field of data analysis, this might be quite daunting.

With so many options, it might be confusing to decide which function to utilize for a certain Excel project.

The most helpful Excel features are the ones that disguise their complexity. The good news is that the basic set of Excel tools can meet the demands of the vast majority of users.

The most basic Excel functions are covered in this topic.

Now function

In an Excel spreadsheet, the NOW function displays the current system date and time. This function just returns the system date and time on the system it is being used in and does not accept any arguments. This function can be used in the following manner, which is quite simple: =NOW ().

Consider the scenario when we want a worksheet to include the current date and time. We can employ the NOW feature. Every time the worksheet is recalculated or opened, the date and time are updated.

Time function

A DATE/TIME function returns the current system date and time, and Excel's NOW function falls under this category. We may examine and interact with the date and time values in formulas thanks to the NOW Excel function in the DATE/TIME category.

The Excel DATE/TIME functions include the TIME Function. We can construct a time using distinct hour, minute, and second components with the aid of TIME.

We might want to date a report while performing a financial analysis. In these circumstances, TIME can be used to transform a text string into a format that indicates the time in decimal form. Additionally, the function can be used to combine different values into a single time value.

This function can be used in the following manner, which is quite simple: =TIME (hour, minute, second).

The following arguments are used with the TIME function:

- ***Hour (mandatory argument): This can indicate the hour and ranges from 0 (zero) to 32767. If a value is greater than 23, it must be divided by 24 and Excel will use the result as the value for the hour.***
- ***Minute (mandatory argument): The minutes are represented by an integer between 0 and 32767. A value is converted to hours and minutes if it is greater than 59.***
- ***Second (mandatory argument): It represents the seconds and can range from 0 (zero) to 32767. A value is converted to hours, minutes, and seconds if it is greater than 59.***

The TIME function returns a decimal number between 0 (zero) and 0.99988426, which represents the times from 0:00 (12:00 AM) to 23:59:59. (11:59:59 P.M.).

4.3 Logical Functions

Excel has built-in logical functions that can be used to do logical operations on Excel data. Logical functions are mostly used to compare pieces of information. MS Excel has many logical functions, such as AND, XOR, OR, NOT, FALSE, TRUE, etc.

These functions are handy when you need to compare numerous variables in a single formula or check for the presence of several different conditions. When their arguments are evaluated, Excel's logical functions do the same as logical operators and return either TRUE or FALSE.

To assist you in selecting the appropriate formula for a given assignment, there is a brief description of the various logical functions available.

AND Function

Description: If the given conditions are all true, return TRUE.

Formula Example: = AND(B2>=10, C2<5)

Formula description: If the value in cell B2 is higher than or equal to 10 and the value in cell C2 is less than 5, the formula will return TRUE; otherwise, it will return FALSE.

OR Function

Description: If any of the inputs evaluate to True, then it returns TRUE.

Formula Example: =OR(A2>=10, B2<5)

Formula description: If either A2 or B2 is larger than 10, or if both are less than 5, then the expression will evaluate as TRUE. The formula will result in FALSE if both conditions are not met.

NOT Function

Description: Send the result of the evaluation backward. For instance, if the condition is false, the result will be TRUE. If the condition is true, the result will be FALSE.

Formula Example: =NOT(A3<=15)

Formula description: If the value in cell A3 is greater than or equal to 15, the result will be TRUE. FALSE is returned if the value is greater than or equal to 15.

XOR Function

Description: Obtains an Exclusive or of all inputs in logical form.

Formula Example: =XOR(A2>=10, B2<5)

Formula description: If A2 is larger than or equal to 10 and B2 is less than or equal to 5, then the expression will evaluate as TRUE. The formula will evaluate to FALSE if any of the two conditions is not met, or if both conditions are met.

4.4 Statistical Functions

Before we go into Excel's statistical functions, it's important to define what we mean by "statistics" and why we require their use. Therefore, statistics is a subfield of science that endows a sample with a characteristic. The process includes data collection, organization, analysis, and presentation.

The statistical functions in Excel span from the simple mean, median, and mode to the intricate statistical distribution and probability tests.

The COUNT function, COUNTBLANK function, COUNTA function, and COUNTIFS function are some of the basic statistic functions.

COUNT function

To count the number of cells that contain a number, use the COUNT function. One thing to always keep in mind is that it will simply count the number.

Syntax

= COUNT(value1, [value2] ...)

Example

The COUNT function is used in an example for you to fully understand it, and one is provided below for you to test out:

This function was used in the example below to count the cells in the range A1:A10, and the output was 8.

We have a logical value in cell A3 and a text in cell A7. COUNT has disregarded both cells.

AVERAGE Function

The AVERAGE Function comes under the category of statistical functions. This function returns the mean value of the entered set of numbers. This function is used to determine the arithmetic mean of a set of inputs.

The function is helpful to a financial analyst in determining the average (mean) of a set of statistics. For instance, we can discover the average revenue for a company over the previous 12 months.

Syntax

=AVERAGE(number1, [number2] ...)

The following arguments are used by the function:

- ***The initial number of the cell reference or range for which the average is desired.***
- ***These are the cell references, extra figures, or a range that we wish to calculate the average for. There is a limit of 255 numbers.***

4.5 Conditional Functions

COUNTIFS

Excel's 'Countif' function determines how many cells meet one or more criteria. This COUNTIFS has the potential to manage time-, money-, text-, and other variable-dependent parameters. COUNTIFS supports the use of logical operators (>,>,=) and wildcard characters (?,*) for selective matching.

Syntax for the COUNTIFS function:

=COUNTIFS (range 1, criterion 1), [range 2, criterion 2],..., range n, criterion n.

Parameters:

- ***Firstly, the range of a cell can be evaluated using criterion 1.***

- ***1st criterion: The parameters by which the set of cells to be included in the final result is narrowed down.***
- ***One range is compared to another, and so on, all the way up to range n. There is the possibility of doing so. The set of cells to which further criteria2,..., criteria n should be applied. There are 127 possible levels of detail.***
- ***Criterion 2, through criteria n: There's no pressure to do it. It is used to determine which cells will be considered in the final output. Extending criterion 2 against the second range, then extending criterion 3 against the third range, and so on. The total parameterization space is 127.***
- ***The COUNTIFS function provides a measurable result.***

4.6 How to Apply a Function Correctly

Function Insertion

Each function has the same configuration. SUM, for example (B1:B4). This function's name is SUM. We are giving the A1:A4 range to excel according to the part between the parentheses (arguments). Using this function, the cells' labels—A1, A2, A3, and A4—are appended. It can be challenging to remember which function to use for a certain task and which arguments to utilize. Excel's insert function functionality will help you, thankfully.

To insert the function, follow the instructions below

- ***Pick a cell to work on.***
- ***From the dropdown menu, choose the insert function.***

The dialog box of "Insert function" appears.

- ***Start by looking for a function or selecting one from a category. Choose COUNTIF, for example, from the statistical categorization.***
- ***Select ok.***
- ***The "Function parameters" dialogue box appears.***
- ***Select the A1:C2 set by clicking on it in the range box.***
- ***In the criterion window, enter >5, then click OK.***

Therefore, COUNTIF determines how many cells in a row are higher than 5.

Instead of selecting the Insert function option, begin typing =COUNTIF (A1:C2, ">5"). When one arrives to =COUNTIF, choose the range A1:C2 rather than typing A1:C2.

Copy the answer rather than typing it again in various cells.

Once you've entered a formula into a cell, there is no need to repeat the process. To move the formula to nearby cells, begin dragging the fill handle (a little square in a cell's lower right corner). To apply the formula to the entire column, position the cursor above the fill handle and double-click the plus sign.

Discard the formula but retain the outcome

A measured value is also deleted when one presses the delete key to erase a formula. However, you should only remove the formula and leave the result in the cell.

This is how you do it:

- ***Select all cells for the formulas.***
- ***Press Ctrl + C to duplicate the selected cells.***
- ***Right-click the selection and select "Paste values from values" to re-paste the computed values into the selected cells. Alternately, to use the unique shortcut for pasting, press Shift+F10, followed by V.***

Operator Priority

In Excel, the order of the calculations is predetermined by default. A formula's contained parts will be computed first if they are in brackets. It then does division and multiplication calculations. Following this, Excel will add and then deduct the remaining formula components Excel multiplies the numbers (A1*A2) to begin. Excel then updates this result to include the information from cell A3.

Excel instead calculates the component included in brackets (A2+A3) first. The quantity in cell A1 is then multiplied by the result.

Avoid Enclosing Amounts in Dual Quotes

Every text in the Excel formulas must be accompanied by "quotation marks." Do not use quotation marks if one does not want Excel to treat numbers as text values. For instance, one could use the formula below in cell C2 to check the value in cell B2 and return 1 if it is "Passed" and 0 if it is not:

B2="pass," 1, 0), =IF

The other cells will contain a column of 1s and 0s that can be measured easily if the formula is copied to them.

If the numbers are double-quoted, what will happen?

When B2="pass","1","0,"

At first look, the output appears to be normal because it has the same column of 1s and 0s. Even still, a closer look reveals that the cell values produced are almost entirely left-aligned, which suggests that they are numeric strings rather than actual numbers. After then, anyone attempting to quantify the 1s and 0s may find themselves pulling their flesh off in an attempt to understand why a perfectly correct SUM or COUNT calculation returns zero.

Copy/Paste the Formula

When a formula is copied to a new cell, Excel modifies the cell references for each new cell. To comprehend this better, take the steps listed below.

The formula in cell A4 should be entered. To copy a cell, right-click it and select Copy (or CTRL + C)

Then, hold CTRL + V and right-click cell B4 before selecting Paste from the Options for paste menu.

You can also drag the formula to cell B4. Click on the bottom right corner of cell A4 to select it, and then drag it to cell B4 by clicking on the lower right corner of cell A4. This takes far less time and achieves the same effects.

As a result, the calculation in cell B4 makes use of the numbers in column B.

Verify that Automatic is selected under Calculation Options.

Excel formulas that suddenly ceased updating automatically most likely had their calculation choices changed to manual. Choose the Formulas tab, go to the Calculation group, and choose Automatic from the Calculation Options tab to fix this.

Chapter 5: Data Entry

Data entry is the process of adding information from one place to another, usually by typing it into a computer program.

5.1 Data Organizing

There are many features in Microsoft Office Excel that make it easy to manage and analyze data. To get the most out of these features, you need to organize and format the data in a worksheet according to the rules below.

Data organization guidelines

Put similar things in the same column. Set up the data so that similar things in the same column appear in all rows.

Keep a range of data separate from other data on the worksheet by leaving at least one empty column and one empty row between the two. When you sort, filter, or add automatic subtotals, Excel will be able to find and choose the range more easily.

Don't put important data to the left or right of the range, because the data might be concealed when you filter the range. Instead, put important data above or below the range.

Don't leave rows or columns blank in a range. Don't leave rows or columns blank in a range of data. Do this so that Excel will be able to find and choose the related data range more easily.

Show all rows and columns in a range. Before making changes to a range of data, ensure that any hidden columns or rows are shown. When columns and rows in a range are not shown, it is possible to delete data by accident.

Data format guidelines

Use column labels to identify data. To make column labels, change the format of the data in the first row of the range of data. Excel can then use these labels to make reports, find data, and set it up in a way that makes sense. Use a different font, format, alignment, border, pattern, or capitalization style for column labels than you use for the data in the range. Before you type the column names, format the cells as text.

Cell borders are used for separating data. If you want to put lines below labels to separate them from data, don't use dashed lines or blank rows. Instead, use cell borders.

Don't put spaces at the start or end of a cell to indent data. This will help you avoid making mistakes. These extra spaces can change how a cell is sorted, searched for, and formatted. You don't have to type spaces between pieces of information. Instead, the Increase Indent command can be used.

Formulas and Formats are kept consistent when new rows of data are added to the climax of a data range. This is done by Excel. If you want to extend a format, three of the five cells before must use the same format. For a formula to be extended, it must be consistent with all of the formulas that came before it.

Use an Excel table layout to work with related data. A range of cells on the worksheet that are next to each other can be turned into an Excel table. Data that is defined by the table can be changed without affecting data outside of the table, and you can quickly filter, sort, calculate or total the data in the table by using specific table features. You can also use tables to keep related sets of data separate by putting them in different tables on the same worksheet.

5.2 Data Filtering

The filter in Excel helps show the right data by temporarily hiding the ones that aren't important. Based on the given criteria, the data is filtered. Filtering lets you focus on the most important parts of a dataset. For instance, a company's sales data by city can be filtered by location. So, the user can see how much money was made in certain cities at a certain time.

When working with a large database, you have to have a filter. A filter is a common tool that turns a large view into one that is easy to understand. To use filters, the dataset must have a header row that says what each column is called.

5.3 Find and Replace

Sometimes you'll need to find a word or number in your spreadsheet, but you're not certain where it is. With just a few clicks of the mouse, Excel's Find and Replace commands can search a worksheet for labels and values.

Find Text

With the Find feature, it's easy to look for certain words and numbers in a worksheet.

- ***On the Home tab, click the Find & Select button.***
- ***Choose Find.***
- ***The Find tab present on the Find and Replace dialog box shows up.***
- ***In the Find what box, type the text you want to find.***
- ***Tap Find Next.***
- ***Excel goes to the first place where the phrase, word, or value you entered is found.***
- ***Press the Find Next button afterward to see more matches.***
- ***When you're done, click Close.***

Replace Text

Now, if you need to change a word that appears in many cells of a spreadsheet, don't change it one cell at a time. Instead, use Replace.

- ***On the Home tab, click the Find & Select button.***

- ***Select Replace.***
- ***The Find and Replace dialog box shows the Replace tab.***
- ***In the Find what box, type the text you want to change.***
- ***In the Replace with box, type the text you want to use instead.***
- ***Click the button Find Next.***
- ***Click on any of these:***
    - ***Replace All: Change every time the item shows up.***
    - ***Replace: Change the item that was chosen.***
    - ***Find All: Look for every instance of the thing.***
    - ***Find Next: Find the item's next instance.***
- ***When you're done, click Close.***

5.4 Sort

Sorting data is any process that involves putting it in an order that makes it simpler to analyze, or see. Sorting is a common way to make research data easier to see and understand. Sorting can be done on raw data (all records at once) or aggregated data (in a chart, table, or some other summarized or aggregated output).

Data is usually put in ascending or descending order by counts, actual values, or percentages, but it can also be put in order by the variable value labels. They are a type of metadata that can be found in some programs. They let the researcher store labels for each possible answer to a categorical question. Most software programs also let you sort by more than one factor.

This kind of sorting is done in a variable order that has already been set. For example, a data set with fields for region and country can be sorted first by region as the primary sort, and then by country. In each sorted region, the county sort will be used.

5.5 Paste Special

Do you know that you can do more in Excel than just copy and paste the whole thing? For example, you can paste only the Value, Column Width, Formula, Formatting, or Comment.

With paste specials, you can choose what you want to put in the cells. When standard copy/paste doesn't give the right results, Excel's Paste special gives a wide range of options from which to choose special elements and mathematical elements.

For example, if we do a calculation in a cell and then want to copy and paste just the result in the same cell or somewhere else in another sheet, or if we want to copy and paste just the column width or just the comments, or if we want to switch the order of the data, or if we want to create a link between cells or between sheets, etc., we can do all of these things.

How to use paste special

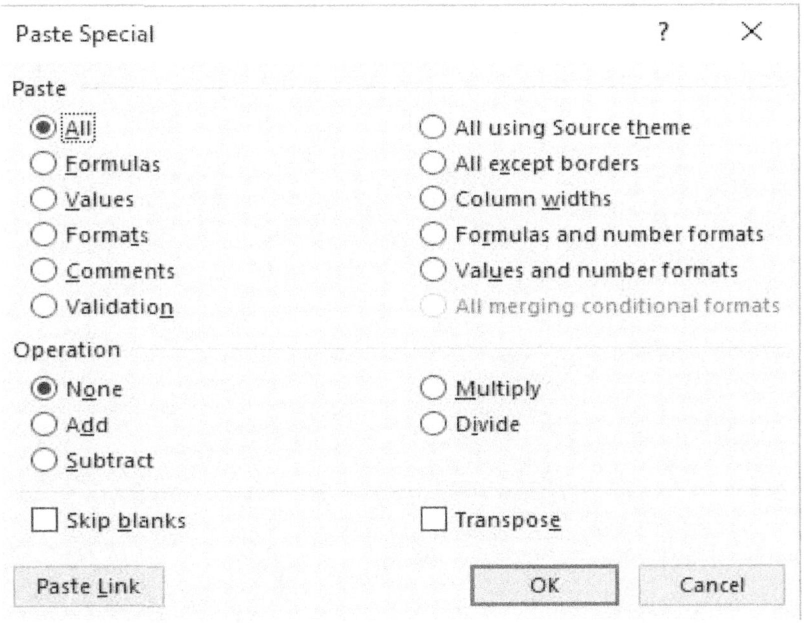

- ***Copy the cells or range from the source. (Press Ctrl+C as a short-cut)***
- ***Select destination cell***
- ***Go to Home > Paste > Paste Specials (use the keyboard shortcut Ctrl+Alt+V).***
- ***Pick the option you want, then click OK or press Enter.***

Yes! It's as easy as copying and pasting.

Chapter 6: Advanced Data Entry

Most individuals use the tried-and-true method of entering data into Excel spreadsheets, which involves going through each cell and row in turn. Using a specialized data entry form can make the process more user-friendly and quicker. It will allow you to view records one by one without having to scroll horizontally.

6.1 Excel Data Entry Form

The data entry process can be made much quicker, more user-friendly, and less prone to errors, especially in large worksheets, by using a customized form in Excel.

When creating an Excel table, how do most people fill it in? By directly inputting information into cells; there are times when you need to scroll up to see the column heads and other times when you need to scroll to the right and then back up to the top of the table. It's easy to accidentally insert data into the wrong cell when working with massive datasets.

To save time, you can request that Excel show you just one row of data in a dedicated input box. A new record can be added here, and existing ones can be updated or edited precisely. Data Validation allows you to establish rules that will be used to approve data entry based on whether or not it satisfies those rules.

Excel Online doesn't have functionality for data entry forms, however, Excel 365, Excel 2016, Excel 2019, Excel 2007, and Excel 2010, do.

Adding the Form tool to Excel

The Excel ribbon does not currently have the Data Form feature. Putting it on the Quick Access menu is the first step in making it readily available.

The form can be added to the QAT in the following ways:

- ***You can access additional commands for the QAT by clicking the arrow down in its upper-right corner.***
- ***On the resulting Excel Options dialogue box, go to the tab labeled "Choose commands from," and either "All Commands" or "Commands Not in the Ribbon" will appear.***
- ***Find the Form command in the left-hand menu and click it. Then select it with the mouse.***
- ***To add the Form to your QAT commands on the right, click the Add button in the center.***
- ***It's as simple as clicking OK to have the modifications applied and the window closed.***

As soon as you add the Form, a button to access it will appear in the Quick Access Toolbar of all of your open spreadsheets.

You may not think you've overcome the biggest obstacle, but you have. With Excel's Form tool installed, you can quickly and easily make a data entry form for any table in your workbook, whether it's brand new or already exists.

6.2 Creating a New Entry Form

Instructions for adding a new record in Excel's Data Entry Form are provided below.

- ***Simply pick a cell at random and click on it in the Excel Table.***
- ***Select the Form button located in the Fast Access Toolbar.***
- ***Fill up the required fields with the appropriate information.***
- ***To add a new record to the table and display a blank form for it, press the Enter key (or select the New button).***

6.3 Navigation Through Existing Records

Data Entry Form allows you to effortlessly navigate and change the records without leaving the dialog box, which is a great time saver.

If your dataset has several columns, this may be extremely helpful. You can avoid a lot of back-and-forth scrolling and effort by doing this.

The following are the procedures for using a data entry form to browse and make changes to the records:

- ***Simply pick a cell at random and click on it in the Excel Table.***
- ***Select the Form button located in the Fast Access Toolbar.***
- ***Use the "Find Next" and "Find Prev" links to move to the next and previous entries, respectively.***
- ***To make a change to a post, type your new text and hit the enter key. If you make a mistake entering data and want to undo it, you can use the "Restore" button.***

To view individual results, utilize the scroll bar.

You can also search for specific information within each record to find what you need quickly.

If you wish to review all the items where the status is "In progress," for instance, you can do so as follows:

- ***Choose a cell at random from the Excel table.***
- ***Select the Form button located in the Fast Access Toolbar.***
- ***Select the Criteria option in the Data Entry Form dialogue box.***
- ***Write "In Progress" in the Status box. This is a case-insensitive value. So, it would still function if IN-PROGRESS were entered.***
- ***You can search for previous and subsequent entries whose state is In-Progress using the Find Prev/Find Next buttons.***

If you have a large dataset and just care about the records that fit a certain set of criteria, a criterion is a great tool to have at your disposal.

Keep in mind that you can filter the results using more than one field of criteria.

To examine only records with the status "In-progress" that were created on or after August 7, 2018, you may set the date filter to ">07-08-2018" and the status filter to "In-progress." If you use the Find Previous/Find Next buttons now, only records with a status of In-progress that have been added after 07-08-2018 will be displayed.

Criteria can also make use of wildcard characters.

If you have entered data inconsistently and have used multiple spellings of a word (such as In progress, in-process, in progress, and in-progress), you will need to employ wildcard characters to get all of the relevant entries.

Specifically, you should perform the following:

- ***Choose a cell at random from the Excel table.***
- ***Select the Form button located in the Fast Access Toolbar.***
- ***To use this feature, select the Criteria button.***
- ***Type "progress" into the Status column.***

You can search for previous and subsequent entries whose state is In-Progress using the Find Prev/Find Next buttons.

In Excel, an asterisk (*) can stand in for any amount of characters; therefore, this works. Therefore, if the status includes the word "progress," the Find Previous and Find Next buttons will recognize it regardless of its position in the list.

Chapter 7: Data Analysis

One of the most sought-after digital skills today is the ability to analyze data. It helps companies look at situations logically and make business decisions based on facts. Microsoft Excel is the most popular business tool for analyzing data. About 750 million people are using Excel right now. No matter how big or small a business is or what services it offers, it uses Excel to do many different things. Eighty to ninety percent of businesses use spreadsheets for forecasting and financial reporting. Capital One and Burning Glass Technologies did a study in 2017 that found that more than 8 out of 10 middle-skill jobs now require Excel skills. When people are interviewed, those with analytical skills get 13–38% more money. So, an extremely desirable combination of Excel skills and data analysis can help send a new job seeker's resume to the top and put middle-skilled workers in a very good position to lead in the future.

7.1 Sorting Data

The term "sort" refers to the process of arranging data into a desired order, such as highest-to-lowest, alphabetical order, or order rows by colors, icons, or custom lists. Multiple columns and row sorting options are available. By sorting, you can locate specific information and arrange it in the desired format. Therefore, it is useful for data visualization and comprehension, which in turn improves the ability to form useful conclusions.

How to Sort Data in an Excel Spreadsheet

To sort a column in Excel, click inside the cell that is at the top of that column.

To see how this works, we'll sort the income column by clicking on cell D3.

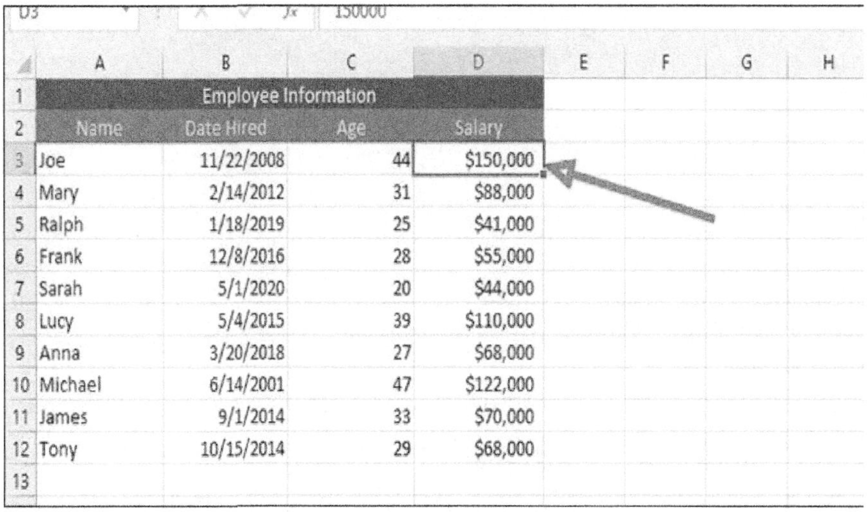

Choose "Filter" from the "Data" tab on the main ribbon's top toolbar.

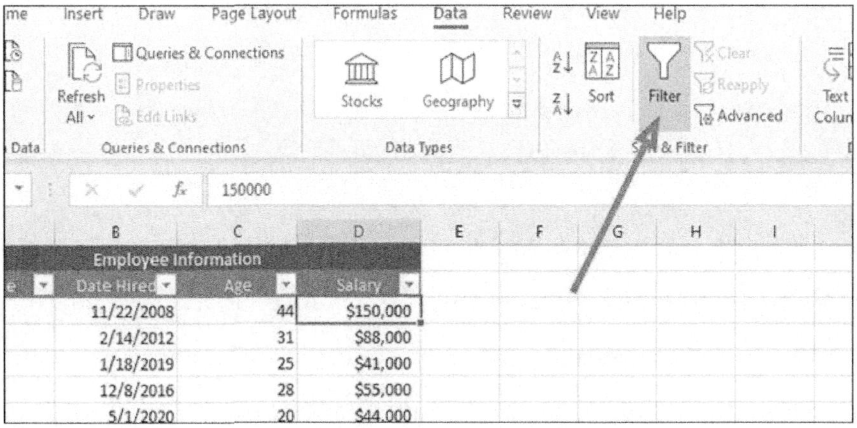

An arrow has been added to the top of each column. Data can be filtered or sorted by clicking the arrow next to the desired column heading.

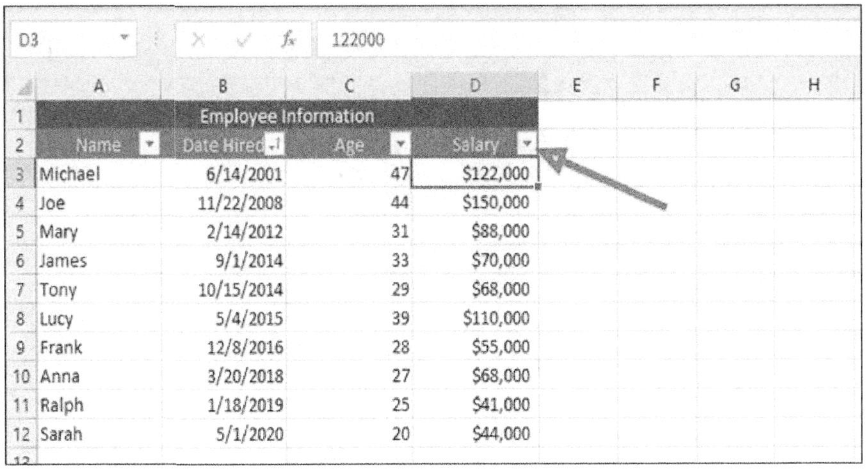

Assuming you have numerical data, the first and most obvious approach to sorting it is from smallest to largest or largest to smallest.

In this situation, we want to order salaries from lowest to highest, so we'll select that choice.

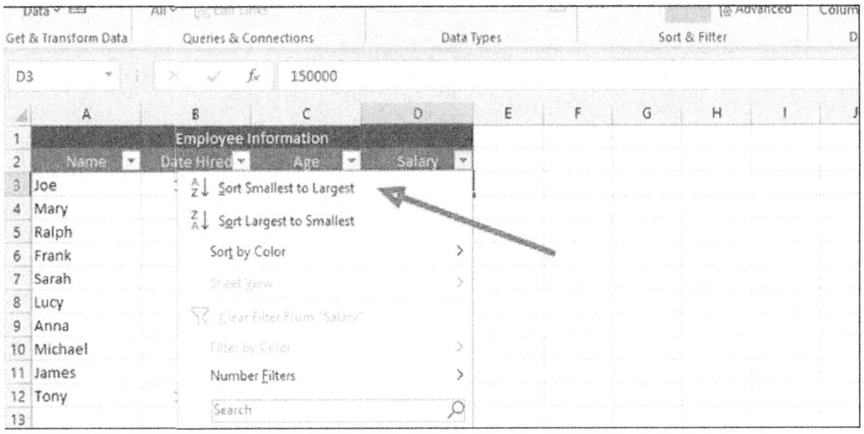

By selecting "Sort Oldest to Newest" in the same menu, we may apply this sorting to any of the other columns, such as "Date of Hire."

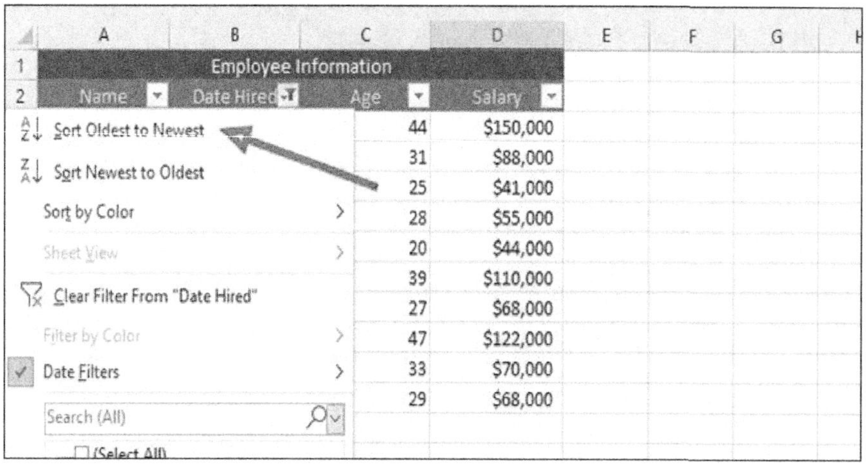

Columns such as "age" and "name" can also be sorted in this way. By using the same arrow and selecting the proper choice, we may arrange the names of employees in any order we like, including, for example, oldest to youngest or alphabetically.

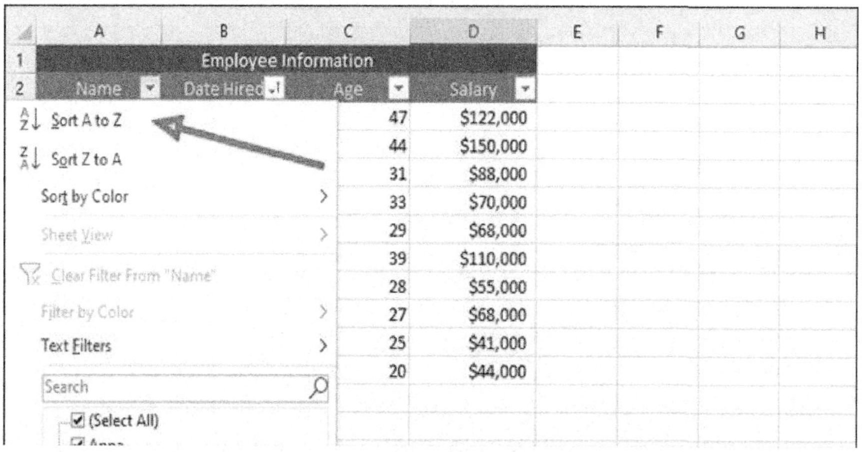

7.2 Filtering Data

It can be time-consuming to locate specific data in a worksheet with hundreds of rows. With the help of filters, you may narrow your data view to only the information that pertains to your inquiry. To further refine your search results, you can use numerous filters at once.

Excel's AutoFilter feature makes it simple to create filters in Excel that are based on the values in a certain column. The arrow next to each column label denotes AutoFilter.

To activate AutoFilter, follow these steps if it is not already active in your sheet: 1. Select the cells you want to filter, click the Data menu's Sort & Filter button (located in the group below the Data tab), and then click Filter.

After applying a filter to a selection of cells or rows and columns, you can undo your changes by clearing the filter. To remove a filter, select it from the drop-down menu adjacent to the column header of the filtered column and then click the AutoFilter button.

How to Filter Data in an Excel Spreadsheet

To see how this works, we'll filter anyone who makes more than $100,000 a year.

To filter this column, click the arrow next to "Salary."

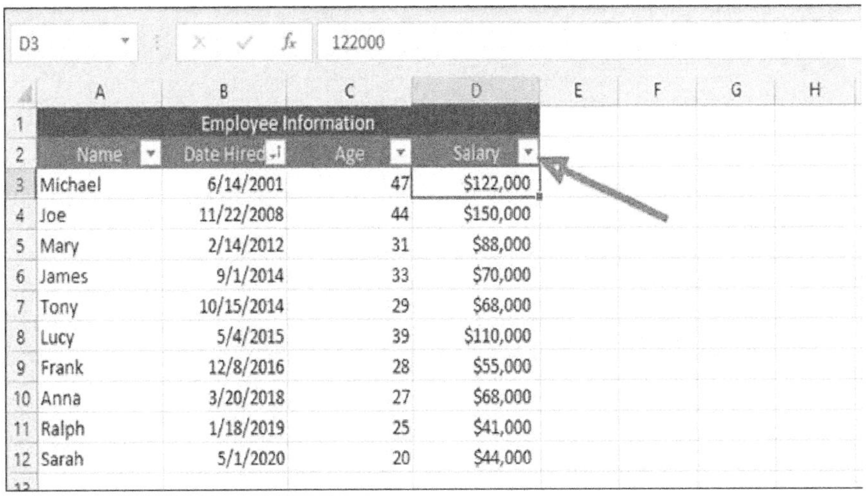

D3 | 122000

Employee Information			
Name	Date Hired	Age	Salary
Michael	6/14/2001	47	$122,000
Joe	11/22/2008	44	$150,000
Mary	2/14/2012	31	$88,000
James	9/1/2014	33	$70,000
Tony	10/15/2014	29	$68,000
Lucy	5/4/2015	39	$110,000
Frank	12/8/2016	28	$55,000
Anna	3/20/2018	27	$68,000
Ralph	1/18/2019	25	$41,000
Sarah	5/1/2020	20	$44,000

Because this list is short, there are a few ways we can do this. The first way, which works perfectly in our example, is to uncheck each individual who earns more than $100,000 and then press "OK." This will take three items off our list so we can see (and sort) only the ones that are left.

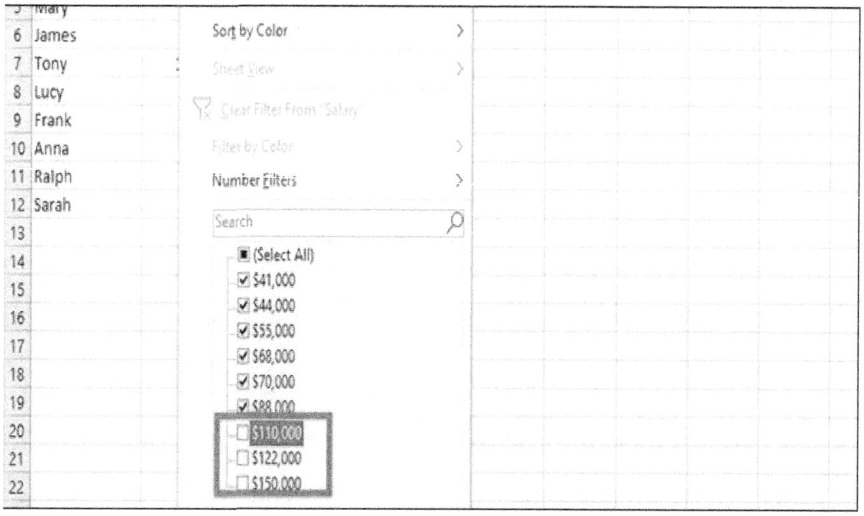

There's something else you can do. Let's click the arrow once more next to "Salary."

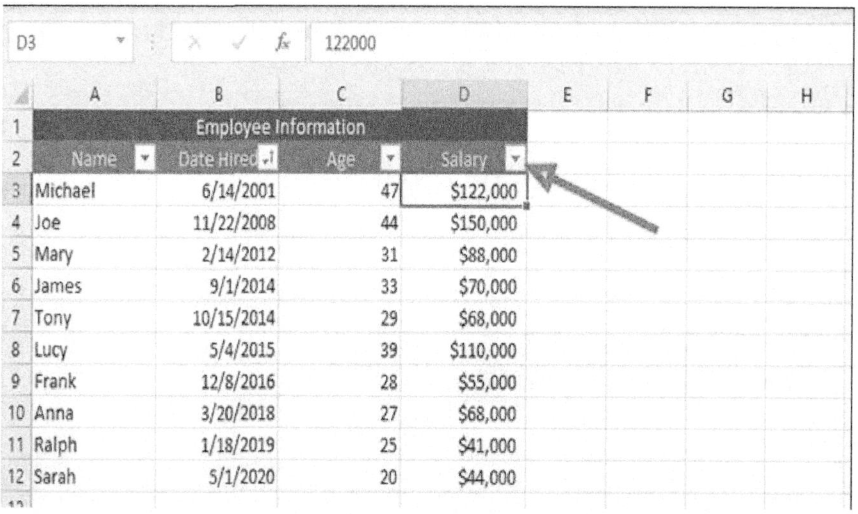

This time, we'll use the filtering menu to choose "Number Filters" and then "Less Than."

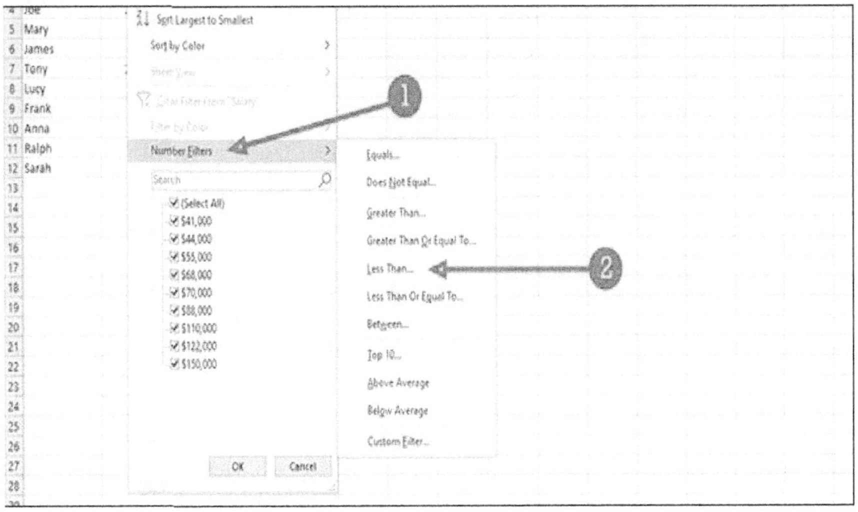

Here, we can also use a filter to get rid of people who make more than $100,000 a year. But this method is much better for large data sets where you may need to click a lot to remove entries by hand. Enter "100,000" (or whatever number you want) to the right of the dropdown box that says "is less than," and then click "OK."

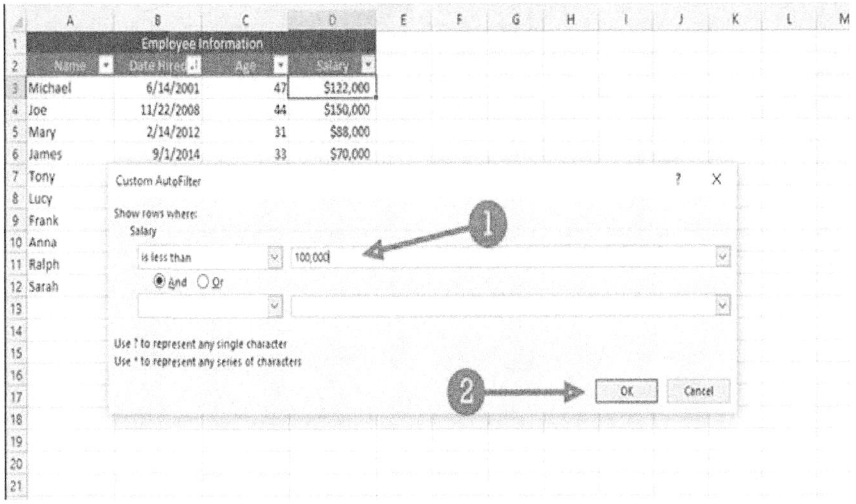

We can also use this filter for many other things. By clicking "Below Average" from the particular menu (Number Filters > Below Average), we can get rid of all salaries that are above average.

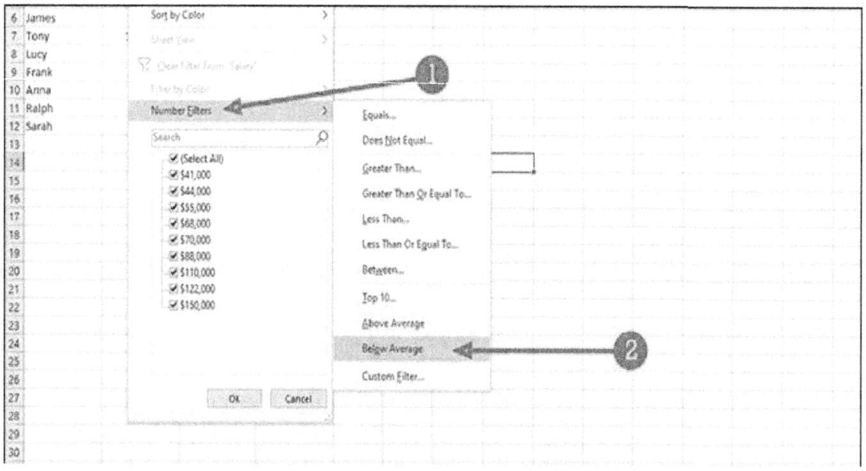

We can also use more than one filter. Here are all the salaries that are more than $60,000 but less than $120,000. First, in the first dropdown box, we'll choose "is greater than."

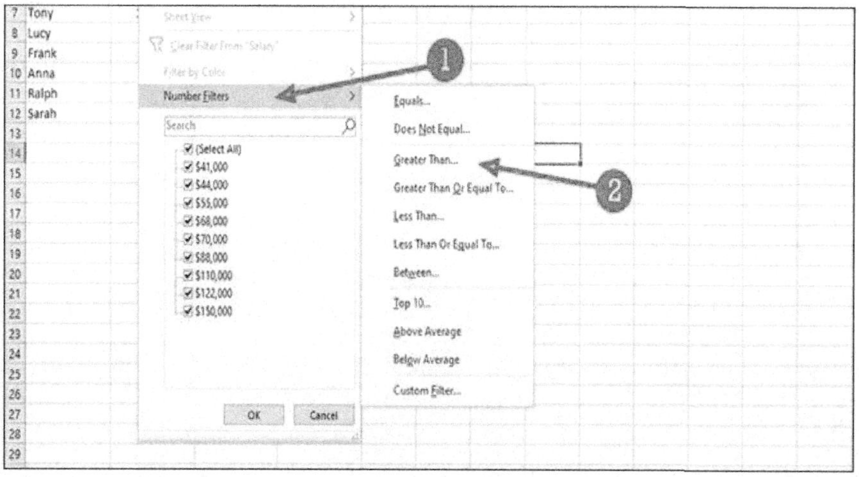

Choose "is less than" from the menu below the last one.

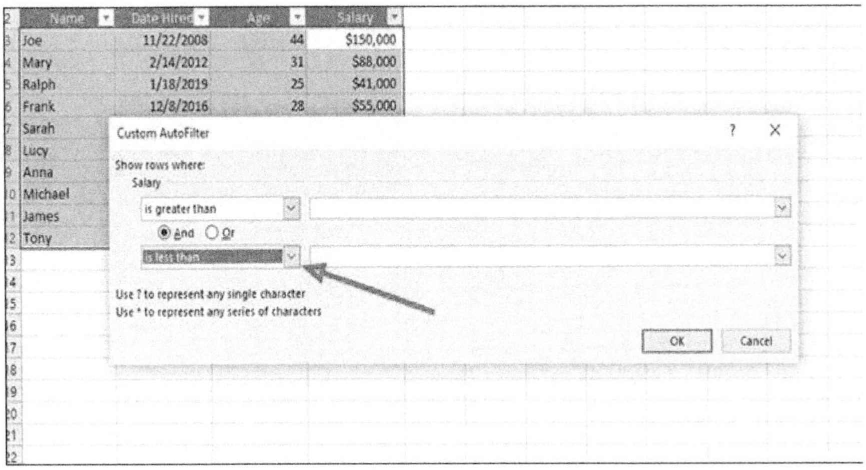

We'll put $60,000 next to "is greater than."

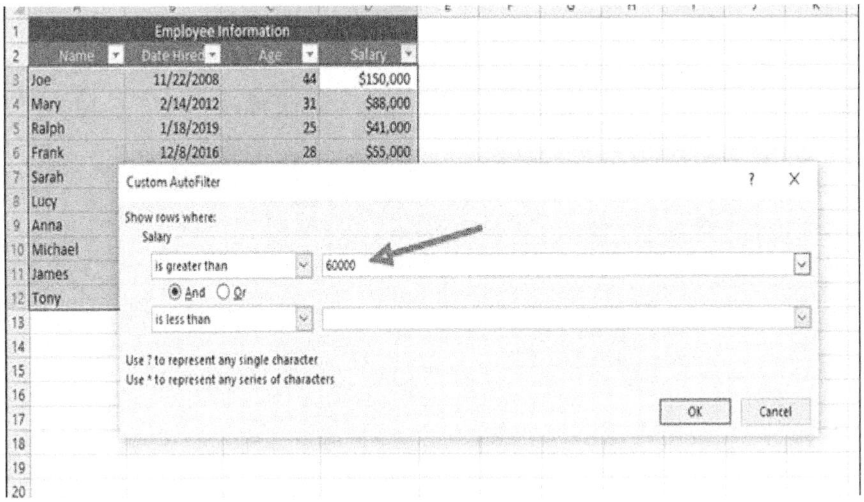

Add $120,000 to "is less than."

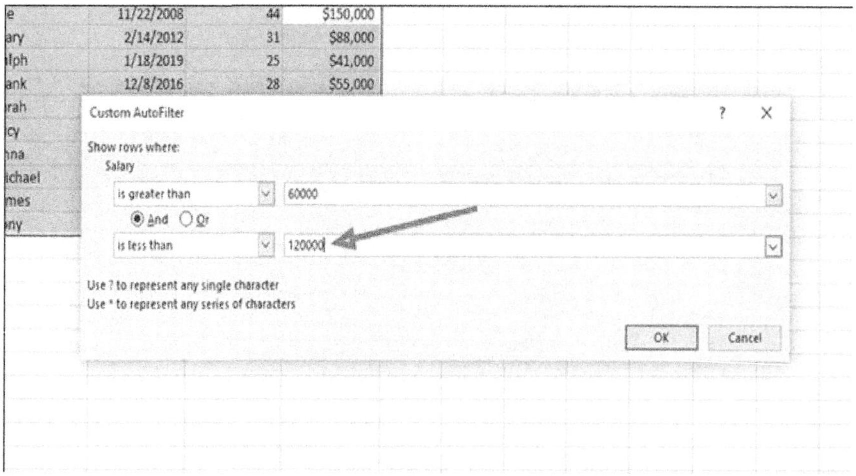

Click "OK" to filter the data so that only salaries between $60,000 and $120,000 are left.

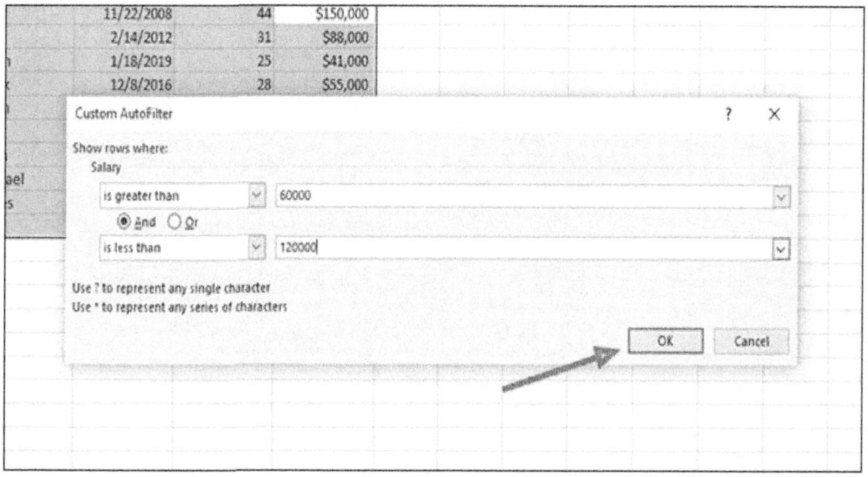

7.3 Remove duplicates

Duplicate information is more likely to show up in bigger datasets. Someone may want to know how many connections they have in an organization. In situations like this, it is important to get rid of duplicates.

To get rid of duplicates, pick the row or column from which you want to remove them. Then, on the data tab, click "Remove duplicates" (underneath tools). A pop-up window would ask you to confirm which information you want to use. Just pick "Remove duplicates," and you're done.

This function can also be used to delete a whole row if the same value is in more than one column. As an example, if someone has three rows of information about a movie but only needs to see one, they can choose all of the datasets and then get rid of the duplicates. The final list can only have certain titles on it, and there can't be any duplicates. Duplicate information is more likely to show up in bigger datasets. Someone may want to know how many connections they have in an organization. In situations like this, it is important to get rid of duplicates. To get rid of duplicates, pick the row or column from which you want to remove them.

Then, on the data tab, click "Remove duplicates" (underneath tools). A pop-up window would ask you to confirm which information you want to use. Just pick "Remove duplicates," and you're done.

This function can also be used to delete a whole row if the same value is in more than one column. As an example, if someone has three rows of information about a movie but only needs to see one, they can choose all of the datasets and then get rid of the duplicates. The final list can only have certain titles on it, and there can't be any duplicates.

Chapter 8: Graphs

Microsoft Excel is a very useful tool for managing and analyzing data that is used by almost every business today. A graph is a design tool in Excel that helps us see how data looks. There are many graphs and charts in Excel that can be used to show data in different ways. This topic will explain the different kinds of graphs you can make in Excel and show you how to do it.

What is a Graph in Excel?

A graph is a visual element on a worksheet that shows data. If you look at a graph in Excel instead of numbers in a dataset, it will be easier to figure out what the data means. Excel has a lot of different graphs you can use to show your data. Excel makes it easy to make graphs.

8.1 How to Create a Graph in Excel

The first step, which is also the most obvious, is to open a blank Excel worksheet or new Excel file.

Done?

Then let's learn how to use Excel to make a graph.

Fill the excel sheet with information

Start by putting the information you need on your Excel sheet.

You can bring this information in from other software, type it in by hand, or copy and paste it.

For example, let's say you own a movie theater in a small town and you often show older movies. You might want to keep track of how many tickets you sell to see which movie is a blockbuster so you can show it more often.

Compare how many tickets were sold in January and February.

Here's what the data might look like:

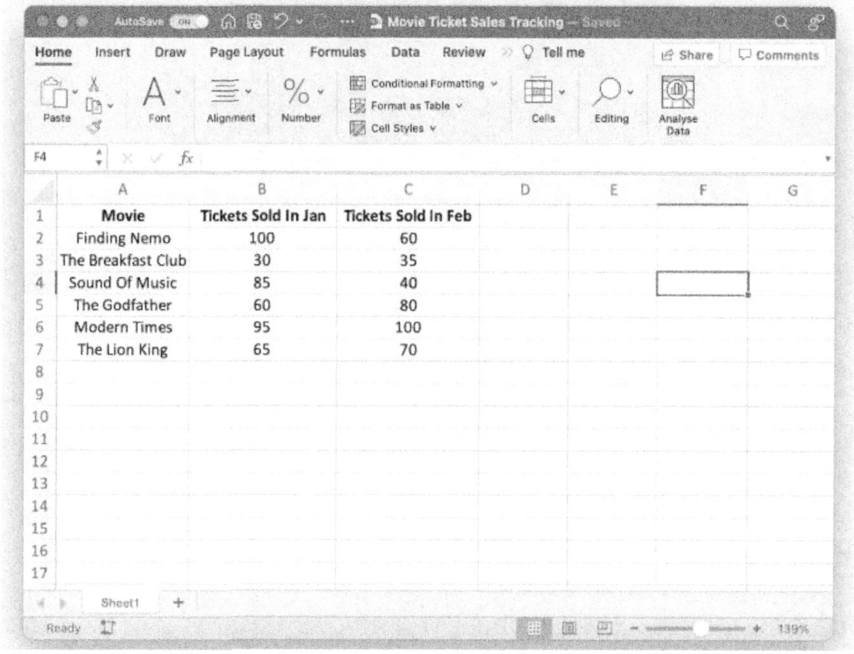

Column A has the names of the movies.

Column B has information about tickets sold in January.

Column C has information about tickets sold in February.

For easier reading, you can make headings bold and center-align your text.

Done? Okay, it's time to choose a graph.

8.2 Selecting the Type of Graph

How you choose a graph will depend on the data you have and how many different things you want to track.

The different types of graphs can be found in the Excel Ribbon, under the Excel Insert tab. They are close to each other, like this:

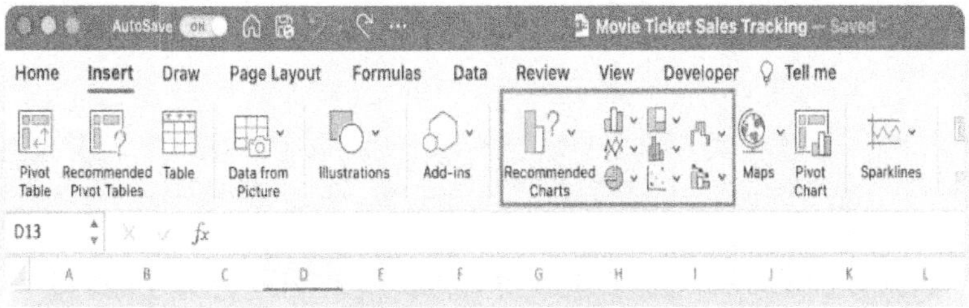

Here are some of the different types of graphs and charts you can use in Excel:

- ***Linear graph***
- ***Bar graph***
- ***Combo graph***
- ***Pie graph***
- ***Scatter plot chart***
- ***Histogram graph***

Let's create a linear graph in excel from the above data

For a line graph to work in Excel, it usually needs two axes, one horizontal and one vertical. You must put the information in two columns.

- ***Step 1: Choose data to make a line graph.***

To select, click and drag from the top left cell (A1) to the bottom right cell (C7) in your ticket sales data. Don't forget to put column headings in.

This will make all the information you want to show in your line graph highlighted.

- ***Step 2: Insert line graph***

After you've chosen your data, you can add the line graph.

Look under the Insert tab for the line graph icon.

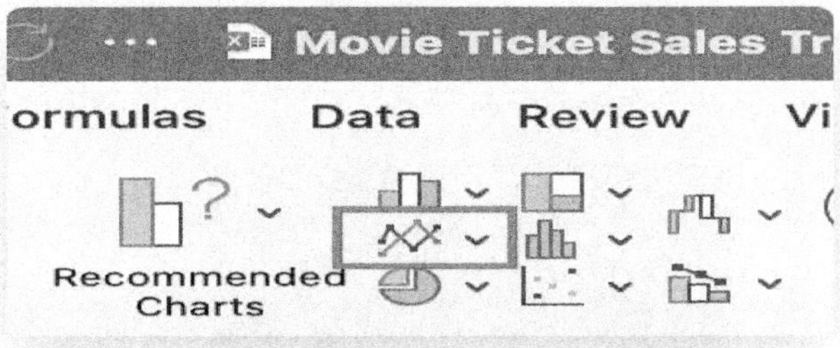

Go to Insert > Line with the data already chosen. When you click on the icon, a dropdown menu will show up where you can choose the kind of line chart you want.

Use the fourth 2-D line graph for this example (Line with Markers).

Excel will add the line graph that shows the data series you chose.

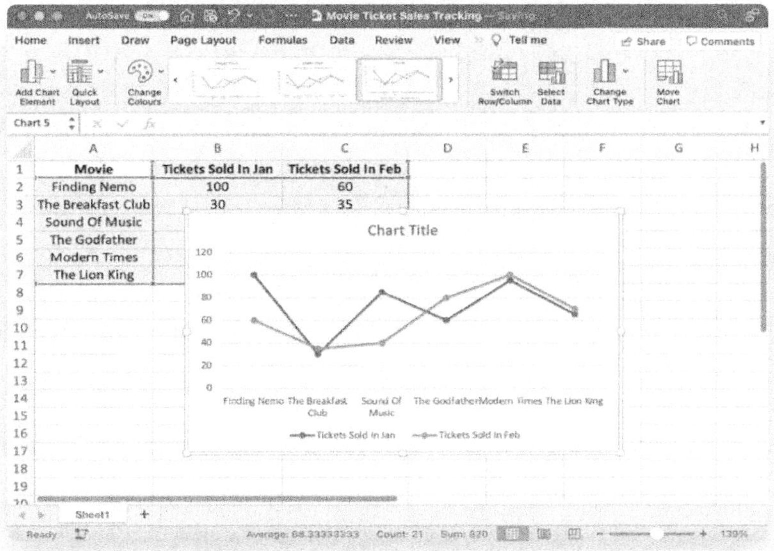

Then, you'll see the names of the movies on the left side of the graph and the number of tickets sold on the right side.

- ***Step 3: Customize your line graph looks***

After adding the line graph, you'll see a new tab on your Excel Ribbon called Chart Design.

Choose the chart style you like and click the Design tab to create the line graph according to your preference.

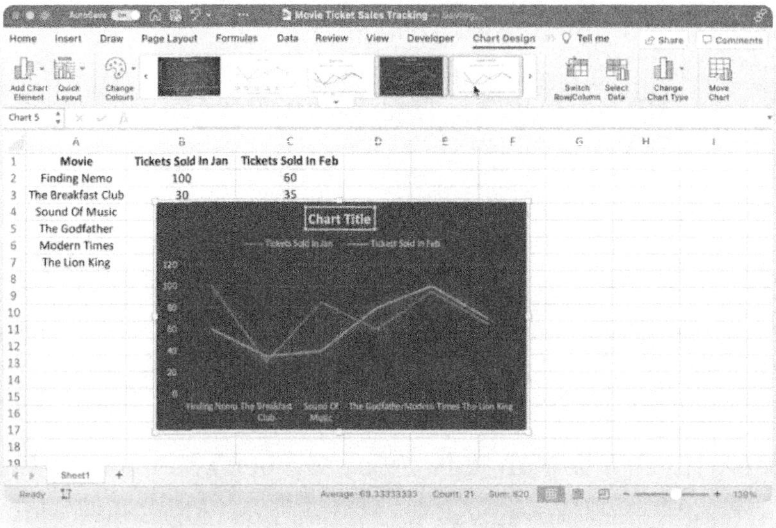

The title of the graph can also be changed.

Choose the Chart Title, double-click to name it, and type in the name you want to use. To save it, click anywhere other than the title box or the chart area.

Let's call this graph "Movie Tickets Sales."

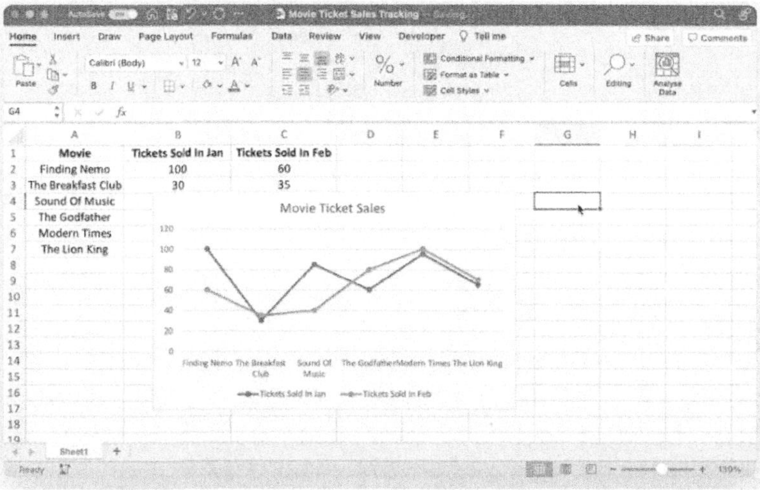

Do you need to change anything else?

If you see something wrong, now is the time to fix it.

Here, for example, The Godfather and Modern Times are mixed.

We should give them some room.

How?

You can move any part of the graph until it looks the way you want.

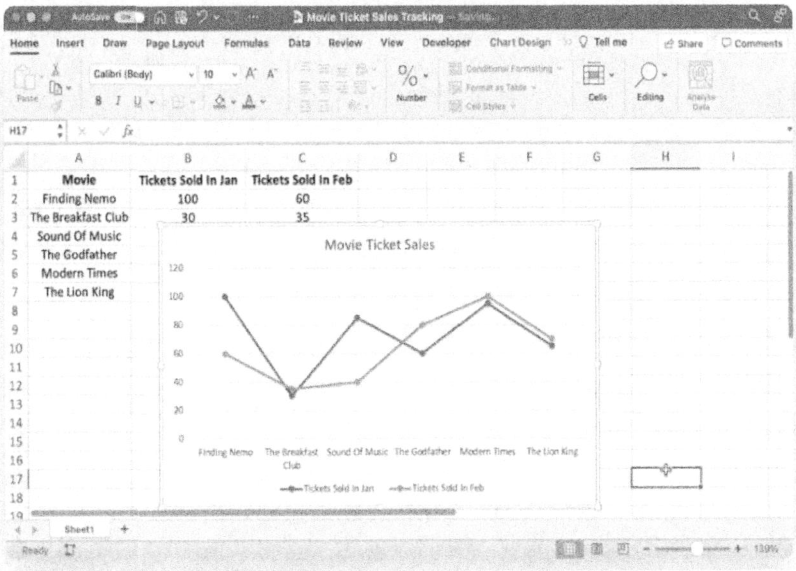

These are merely a few examples. You can change anything about a chart, including the labels on the axes if you want to.

Just double-click on any chart element to open a sidebar with formatting options like this:

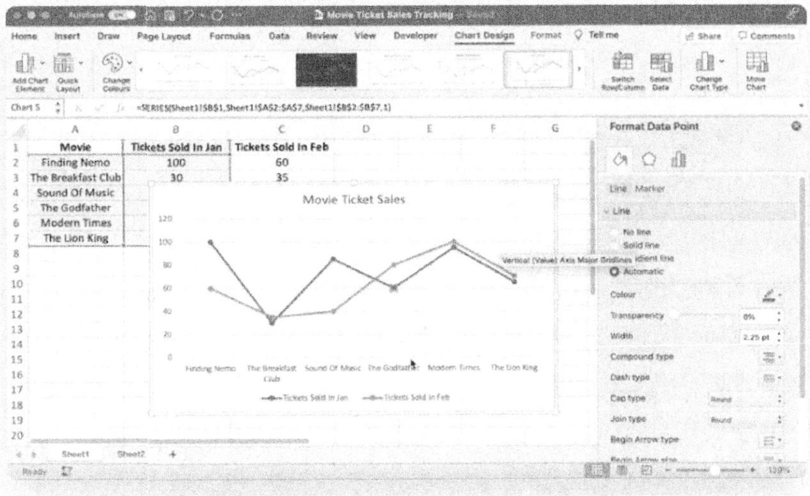

All done! You've made a line graph in Excel.

8.3 Basic Types of Graphs

Linear Graph

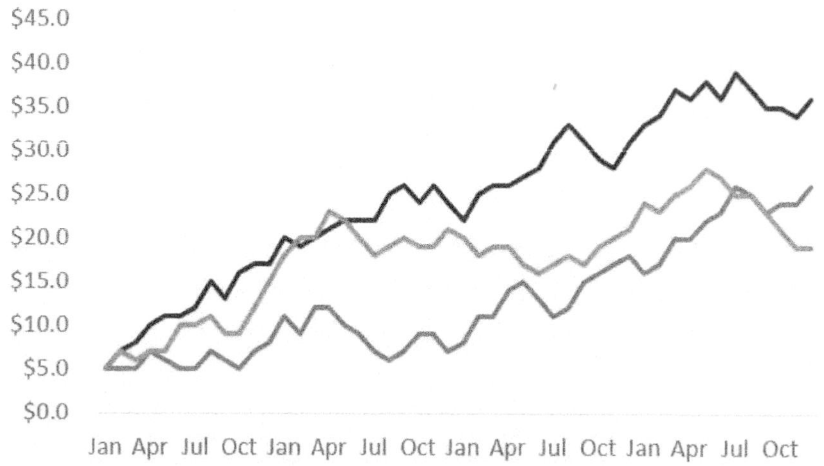

The line graph is the simplest and classic type of chart graph. This is the best way to show multiple sets of data that are closely related to each other. Line graphs are great for a simple look because they only have lines and aren't as complicated as other types of charts, like the ones below.

Bar Graph

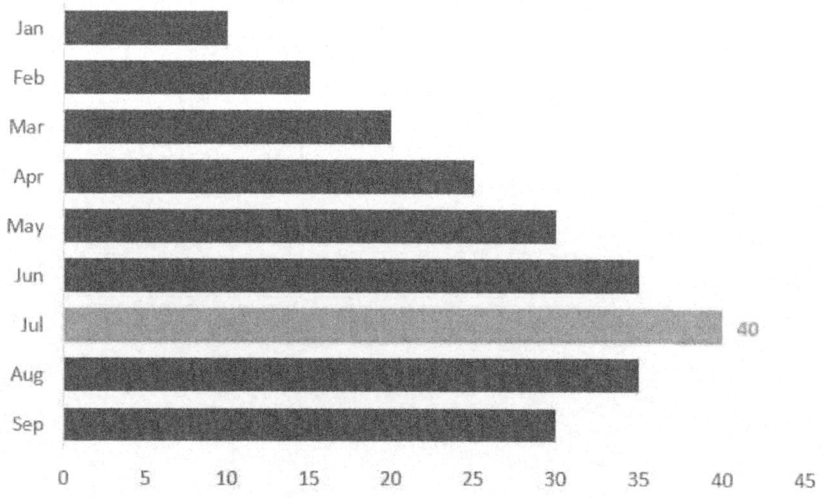

Bar graphs (or column graphs) are the best way to show a single set of data. Bar charts are much heavier than line graphs, so they stand out on the page and make a point.

Combo Graph

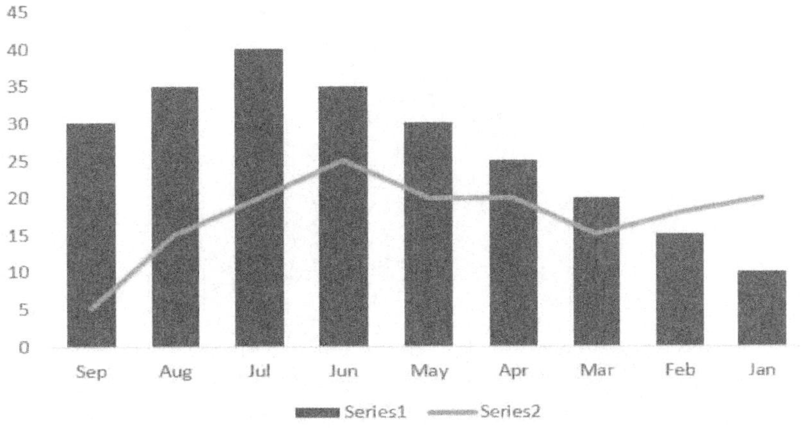

You can make a combo chart with lines and bars by putting together the above two types of graphs. This is a great way to show two sets of data that have very different scales and may be written in different units. Most of the time, dollars are on one axis and percentages are on the other.

Pie Graph

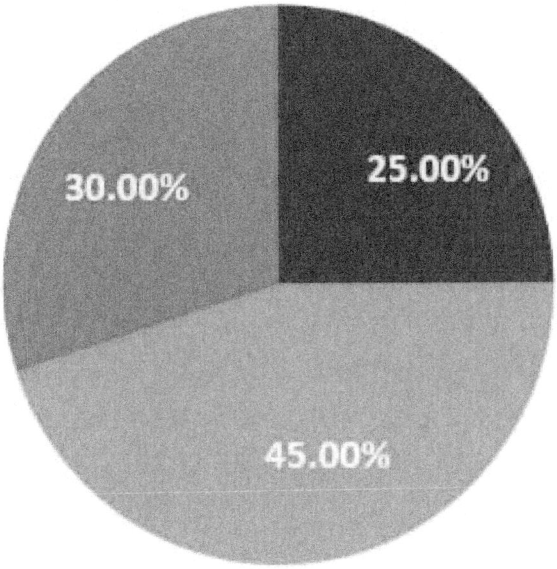

A pie chart is just a circle-shaped graph that shows data in the shape of a pie. It is divided into various parts, and each part is a certain amount of the whole. People don't like pie charts because they are messy and hard to read. But if you want to show how a small number of data points break down by percentage, they can be very useful.

Histogram Graph

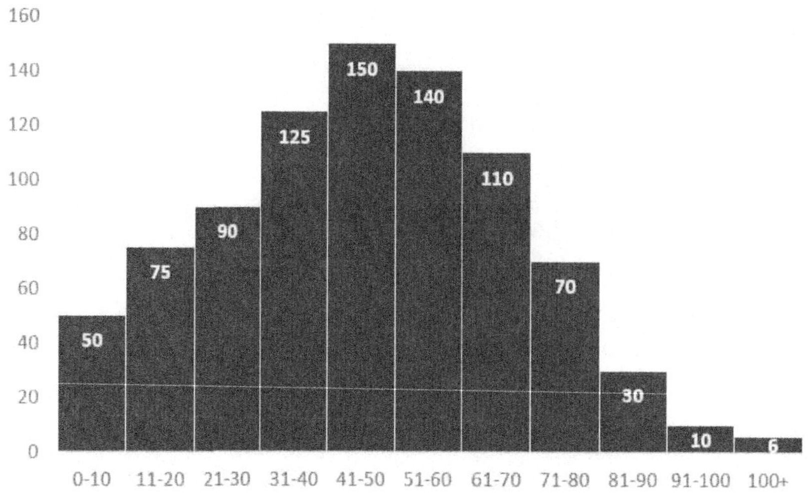

A histogram is a type of graph that shows how a set of data is spread out. They make a graph that shows the percentage or number of times each category shows up. For example, to show how people are spread out by age (0-10, 11-20, 21-30, etc.), we can see which age groups have the most people and how many people are in each one.

8.4 Other Types of Graphs

Financial graphs

Financial graphs and charts are visual tools that help companies track different performance metrics in areas like budgets, liquidity, cash flow, expenses, and others. By doing this, they can handle risks well and make sure their finances are healthy and their growth is steady.

No matter how big a company is, the most important things to do to make sure it runs as well as possible are to do regular financial analytics and make sure the data management is of the highest quality. If the finance department sounds an alarm, everyone must pay close attention because it's about the most important information, and ignoring it could cause serious problems. Because of this, financial charts must be made with the utmost care.

Scatter Plot Graph

A scatter plot graph shows the relationship between two different variables or shows trends in how they are distributed. Use this graph when you have a lot of different data points and want to show how they are similar. This is helpful when looking for outliers or trying to figure out how your data is spread out.

Area Graph

An area graph is a line chart with a color or pattern in the space between the x-axis and the line. It is useful for showing how parts relate to the whole, like how the sales of each sales rep add up to the total sales for the year. It helps you look at both big-picture and personal trends.

Chapter 9: Printing an Excel Worksheet

Microsoft Excel gives you a lot of tools that you can use to make and change your data. You can change the worksheets so that they show the most amount of information possible by using filters, sorting, and making PivotTables and charts.

After you set up your worksheet so that it displays your data in the best way, you can print it out to use in a presentation or report. You can select to print all or a section of any of your worksheets, modify how your data and charts look on the printed page and even hide any error messages that might show up in your worksheets.

This chapter shows you how to get your worksheets ready to print, how to print all or part of a worksheet, how to print charts, and how to add headers and footers to the worksheets.

9.1 Adding Header and Footer to Worksheet

Headers or footers are used to make sure that the same information is at the top or bottom of every printed page. Every printed page has a header and footer.

When you show the headers and footers of your workbook, Excel shows the worksheet in the Page Layout view. It shows you exactly how your worksheet will look when printed. It also lets you make changes to your file, which Print Preview doesn't do.

Excel splits its headers and footers into three parts: the left, the middle, and the right. When you point to a header or footer section that can be changed, Excel highlights that section to show that clicking on it will open it for editing.

When you turn on a header or footer segment, you can add one of the many standard headers and footers, such as page numbers alone or page numbers accompanied by the name of the workbook. The list of headers that shows up depends on how your worksheet and workbook are set up and what is in them.

You can also make your headers by typing in your text or adding a picture, like a company logo, to a worksheet. By adding graphics, you can make it clear that the worksheet is about your company. This is helpful if you use the worksheet in a printed report that is sent to people outside of your company. After you put a graphic in a header or footer, you can adjust it to be bigger or smaller, change how it looks, or add borders.

When you print or show a worksheet, you might require having different headers for even or odd pages, or maybe just for the first page. After you tell Excel you want separate headers, it tells you if a header or footer is for the first page or, if necessary, an odd or even page.

The header and footer of your worksheet will always have the same width as the printed spreadsheet, but you can change their height.

Editing headers and footer

- ***Click Header & Footer in the Text group on the Insert tab of the ribbon.***
- ***Click where you want to change the header or footer.***

Switching between header and footer

- ***Click Header & Footer.***
- ***Click "Go to Footer" to move to the bottom of the page.***

Or,

- ***Click the "Go to Header" button to move to the top of the page.***

Adding text to header and footer

- ***Start editing by opening a header or footer section.***
- ***Click a button in the Header & Footer Elements group on the Design tab of the ribbon. This will add the text you want to your header or footer.***

- ***Type in any extra text you'd like to see in the header or footer.***
- ***Format the text with the tools on the Home tab.***

Adding automated header and footer

- ***Start editing by opening a header or footer section.***
- ***Click the Header button in the Header & Footer group, and then click the header you want to add.***

Or,

- ***Click the Footer button and then click the footer that comes up on its own.***

Adding a graphic to the header and footer

- ***Start editing by opening a header or footer section.***
- ***Click Picture in the Header & Footer Elements group.***
- ***In the dialog box for adding pictures, click from a file.***
- ***Go to the folder where the picture you would like to add is stored.***
- ***Click the file twice.***

Adding a different header for the first page

- ***Click the worksheet's header or footer option.***
- ***Click the Different First Page box in the Options group.***

Different Headers and footers for even and odd pages

- ***In your workbook, turn on a header or footer.***
- ***Click the Different Odd and Even Pages check box in the Options group.***
- ***Show an odd-numbered page and make the header for odd-numbered pages.***

Or,

- ***Show an odd-numbered page and make the header for odd-numbered pages.***

9.2 Prepare Worksheets for Printing

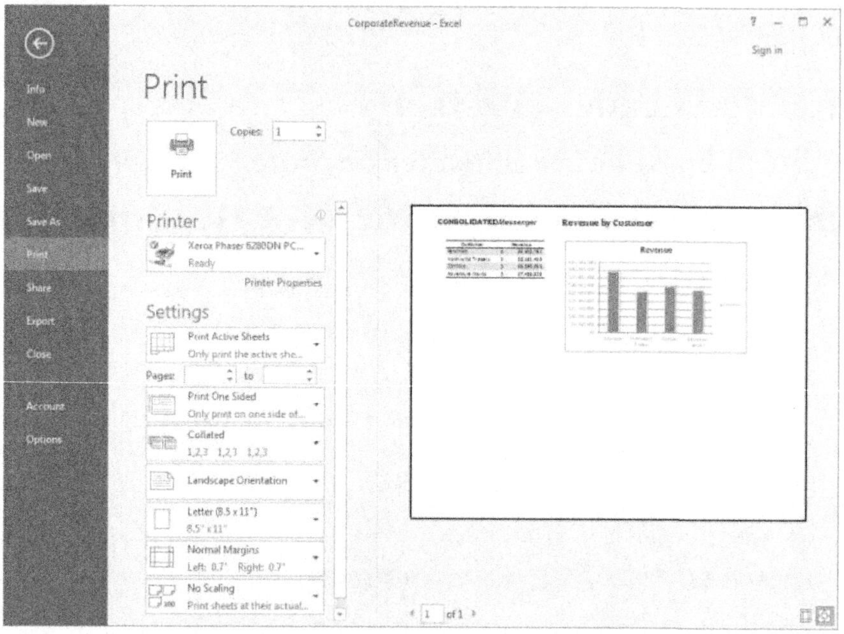

When you're ready to print the worksheet, you can change its properties to make sure that all of your information shows up on the worksheet and that the printing is in the middle of the page. In Excel, all of these printing options are in one place called the "Backstage view."

You can adjust the count of copies to print, the printer you will be sending the file to, whether Excel should print the page in portrait or landscape mode, the paper size to use, the margin settings you want, and whether the worksheet's contents should be scaled to fit on a certain number of printed pages.

Adjusting the worksheet content so that it fits on the printed page

Three margin settings that come with Excel: Normal, Wide, and Narrow. By default, Excel uses the Normal setting, but you can choose any of the other three options or set your margins.

One problem with printing worksheets is that the information on them is often wider than on a normal sheet of paper. If so, you can change how the rows and columns are lined up on the page. When the columns line up with the long edge of the paper, the page is in portrait mode. When the columns line up with the short edge of the paper, the page is in landscape mode. You might get a better fit if you switch between portrait mode and landscape mode.

If you can't fit everything on one page by changing the worksheet's orientation, you can alter its size. When you scale a worksheet to print it, you can choose how many pages it will take up when printed. You can change the size of your worksheet so that everything fits on a certain number of printed pages. You can also choose how many printed pages will be used for columns, rows, or both. If you have a list of data with 100 rows long and 15 columns wide, you could scale it so that all of the columns fit on each page of your printout.

When you glance at the worksheet in the backstage view, you can see how it will look when printed; including how many pages it will be on.

Adjusting page breaks in a worksheet

You can also change where Excel puts its page breaks to change how your worksheet looks when it's printed. At a page break, Excel starts printing the next set of data on a new sheet of paper. You can change these settings directly or indirectly by changing the margins of a worksheet. You can see a worksheet in the Page Break Preview version by clicking the Page Break Preview button on the View tab of the ribbon. In Page Break Preview mode, the page breaks are shown by the blue lines in the window.

A page break can also be moved by dragging it to where you want it. Excel will change the properties of the worksheet so that, if possible, the area you specified will be printed on a single page.

How to create a break between pages on a worksheet

- ***Click the column or row header where you would like to add a page break.***
- ***Click the Breaks button in the Page Setup group on the Page Layout tab of the ribbon, and then click Insert Page Break.***

How to remove page break

- ***Click the row header at the bottom of the page.***
- ***Click the Breaks button in the Page Setup group, and then click Remove Page Break.***

Resetting all page breaks

- ***Click the Breaks button, and then select Reset All Page Breaks.***

Change the order of printing worksheets

When you look at a document in Page Break Preview mode, words in light gray on the worksheet pages show the order in which the pages will be printed. (These markers only show up in Page Break Preview mode; when the document is printed, they aren't there.) You can alter the order in which the pages print if you want to. One reason for changing the order in which Excel prints the worksheet pages is to keep relevant material on consecutive pages.

To change how the pages of a worksheet are printed

- ***Click the dialog box launcher in the Page Setup group on the Page Layout tab.***
- ***Click the Sheet tab in the Page Setup window.***
- ***Choose "Down" and "Over."***

Or

- ***Choose "Over" and "Down."***
- ***Press OK.***

9.3 Print Worksheets

Excel allows you to choose how it prints a worksheet when you're ready to do so. For example, you can select the printer, print duplicates of the worksheet, and choose if the copies are collated or not. You can also print more than one worksheet at once by choosing the worksheet tabs in the tab bar prior you start printing, or you can print the whole workbook at once.

Some of the worksheets you print could be works in progress. If some of the values are missing, the formulas might not work right. Excel lets you choose how to print any errors in your worksheet. You can print the error as it normally appears in the worksheet, print a blank cell in its place, or choose one of two other error messages that are not standard.

Print a single Excel worksheet

- ***Open the worksheet you would like to print up on the screen.***
- ***Click Print in the backstage view's left pane.***

Or

- ***Click CTRL+P***
- ***Choose the options you want the print job to use.***
- ***Select the Print button.***

Print a worksheet more than once

- ***Select Ctrl+P.***
- ***Change the number in the box that says "Copies."***
- ***Click the button that says "Print."***

Printing multiple worksheets

- ***Press and hold the Ctrl key and click on the tabs of the worksheets you want to print.***
- ***Press Ctrl-P.***
- ***Click the button that says "Print."***

Change how Excel prints errors on worksheets

- ***Click the dialog box launcher on the Page Layout tab that is in the Page Setup group.***
- ***Click the Sheet tab in the Page Setup window.***
- ***In the "Cell errors as" drop-down menu, choose the option that matches how you want errors to be printed.***
- ***Press OK.***

9.4 Defining The Parts of Worksheets for Printing

Excel gives you a lot of control over how your worksheets look when you print them. It also gives you a command over which parts of the worksheets will be printed. You can select which pages of a worksheet with more than one page to print, for example. If you only want to print a part of a worksheet instead of the whole sheet, you can define the area or areas you want to print and then use the Center on Page controls present on the Margins tab of the Page Setup dialog box to command Excel how to place the area on the printed page.

If you want to print more than one page of a worksheet, you can have Excel replicate one or more rows at the top of the sheet or columns on the left. When you repeat a row with headers, the data is easier to read throughout the whole printed document. You and your coworkers won't have to go back to the first page to figure out what each row and column contains.

Print out selected pages

- ***Press CTRL+P.***
- ***In the first Pages box on the Print page of the backstage view, type the number of the page you want to print first.***
- ***Type the number of the final page you want to print into the second box that says Pages.***

Defining a print area

- ***Choose the cells you'd like to print.***
- ***Click Print Area in the Print Setup group on the Page Layout tab to see a list of print area options. Then click Set Print Area.***

When you click Print from the backstage view, the preview will show what you chose. After that, you can either print the worksheet or go back to it and repeat the steps to make changes.

Defining a multi-region print area

- ***Choose the first area of the cell that you want to print.***
- ***Hold down the Ctrl key and click on any other cells you want to print.***
- ***Click Set Print Area on the Print Area menu.***

When you click Print from the backstage view, the preview will show what you chose. After that, you can either print the worksheet or go back to it and repeat the steps to make changes.

Remove a printing area

- ***Click any cell in the area that says "Print."***
- ***Click Clear Print Area on the Print Area menu.***

When you click Print from the backstage view, the preview will show what you chose. After that, you can either print the worksheet or go back to it and repeat the steps to make changes.

How to position the printed material where you want it on the page

- ***Click the dialog box launcher in the Page Setup group.***
- ***Click the Margins tab in the Page Setup box.***
- ***Check the box next horizontally to center the print job on the page.***
- ***Or, check the box next vertically to center the print on the page vertically.***

When you click Print from the backstage view, the preview will show what you chose. After that, you can either print the worksheet or go back to it and repeat the steps to make changes.

Print columns over and over on the left side of each page

- ***Click Print Titles in the Page Setup group.***
- ***Click the Collapse Dialog button to the right side of the Columns on the Sheet tab of the dialog box at Page Setup.***
- ***Choose the column headers for the columns you want to repeat on the left side of the page.***
- ***Click the button that says "Expand Dialog"***
- ***Press OK.***

When you click Print from the backstage view, the preview will show what you chose. After that, you can either print the worksheet or go back to it and repeat the steps to make changes.

Print the same rows at the top of each page

- ***Click on Print Titles.***
- ***Click the Collapse Dialog button to the right of the Rows on the Sheet tab of the dialog box at Page Setup to repeat at the top box.***
- ***This will make the dialog box smaller.***

- ***Choose the row headers for any rows you would like to repeat at the top of the page.***
- ***Click the button that says "Expand Dialog"***
- ***Press OK.***

When you click Print from the backstage view, the preview will show what you chose. After that, you can either print the worksheet or go back to it and repeat the steps to make changes.

Chapter 10: Visualization Tricks

10.1 How to Format Tables

Excel tables make it much easier to view and manage data because they have many special features, such as built-in filter and sort options, structured references, calculated columns, total rows, etc.

By turning data into an Excel table, you get a head start on formatting as well. The background colors and font, banded rows, borders, and so on are already set up when you add a new table. If you don't like the default format of a table, it's easy to change it and give Excel tables a unique look. In this topic, you will learn about simple ways to do it.

Use the built-in table styles to make a table look good right away.

Using the built-in Table styles, you can quickly change the way you have newly created Excel Table looks.

- ***Choose any cell in the table Footwork.***
- ***Then press the drop-down arrow next to Table Design > Table Styles.***
- ***Now, select one of the Table Styles that are already built in.***
- ***You can see what each style looks like by moving your mouse over it.***

Change the Theme of the Workbook

The colors in the Table Styles options come from the Office theme that is used by default. One can modify the theme of the Workbook to quickly change the options there:

- ***Go to Page Layout then select themes and from the drop-down of themes choose a theme that is different from the default Office theme.***

To see how changing the theme affects all of the Table Styles options, select a cell in the table, go to Table Tools > Design > Table Styles, and click on the drop-down arrow. This will show you the different color schemes that come from the new theme.

10.2 Changing Gridline Color in Excel

Did you know that you can change the color of the gridlines in Excel? This is a great way to make your worksheets stand out or to use colors to organize them.

Say you have a workbook with several sheets that each represents something different. Modifying the color of the gridlines can help you with your color coding.

Using the "Gridline Color" setting in Excel Options, you can change the color of the gridlines.

- ***If your spreadsheet is already open, choose "File," which is to the left of the "Home" tab.***
- ***After that, click "Options."***
- ***Next, use the menu on the left side of the screen to move to "Advanced."***
- ***Then look for "Display Options for this Worksheet."***
- ***Once you're in the Display Options, choose the tab for which you want to change the color of the gridlines and then pick a color.***
- ***When you click OK, your gridlines will change color.***

10.3 Grouping and Ungrouping Rows and Columns in Excel

If you have a lot of data in your document, it can be hard to read. Fortunately, Microsoft Excel has a feature called "Group" that allows you to organize the data into segments that you can easily show and hide, usually the section you chose to group. If you want to get rid of the segments in your spreadsheet, you can do this.

Grouping rows and columns

- ***Open a spreadsheet that already exists.***
- ***Mark the column or row you want to group.***
- ***On the Data tab, in the upper right corner of the Excel window, click the Outline button.***
- ***Click Group in the Group menu.***
- ***You can choose Columns or Rows from the Group dialog box that pops up. Choose the one you want, and then click OK.***

On the left side of the spreadsheets, there are buttons you can use to hide or show the section you've grouped.

With button 1, you can hide the group section. With button 2, you can show it again. With the (–) button, you can hide the group section, and with the (+) button, you can show it again.

The group segment will be hidden when you click the (–) button.

You can also use another way to group rows and columns in Excel.

You can quickly group a column or a row in your spreadsheet by pressing the Shift, Alt, and Right Arrow keys at the same time.

Ungrouping rows and columns

- ***Mark the row or column you've put together.***
- ***On the Data tab, in the upper right corner of the Excel window, click Outline.***
- ***Click Ungroup, and then choose Ungroup from the drop-down menu.***
- ***A box called "Ungroup" will pop up. Choose a Row or Column and click "OK."***

You can quickly group a row or column in your spreadsheet by pressing Shift, Alt, and the left arrow key at the same time.

Chapter 11: How to Secure Your Work

Excel's protection features allow you to safeguard your work in a variety of ways, such as by requiring a password to start a workbook, restricting access to the entire workbook to only certain users, or locking a worksheet to prevent the accidental deletion of formulas. In this chapter, we will go over the key choices you have when deciding how to secure Excel files.

11.1 Autosaving function

Even though Excel keeps getting better with each new version, it may still crash from time to time (especially if you're working with a large dataset).

And sometimes it's not Excel's fault, like when the power goes out, or your system freezes because of something other than Excel.

Excel has a feature called "AutoSave" that will automatically save your work in these situations so you don't lose your data. Using the AutoSave tool in Microsoft Office, you can temporarily store changes in a database on your local computer. You can change where Autosave saves your game. When a file is stored on OneDrive or SharePoint Online in Microsoft 365, AutoSave is turned on by default.

With AutoSave turned on, Excel will save your file when an unexpected problem happens, like the program crashing, the power going out, or the system getting corrupted. This will make sure that you lose as little data as possible. Now, let's look at how to turn on AutoSave in Excel.

How you can turn on the Autosave feature from the options dialog box

From the Options dialog box, you can set Excel to automatically save changes. Once this is done, it will be turned on for all of your workbooks on that system.

AutoSave is only for Office365 users, so keep that in mind. You can only use Auto Recover if you don't have Microsoft 365.

Here's what you need to do to turn on Auto-save in Excel:

- ***Click the "File" button.***
- ***Choose Options***
- ***Click the Save button on the left side of the Excel Options box.***
- ***Check the box next to the option "Save Auto Recover information every." The value is set to 10 minutes by default, but you can change it if you want to.***
- ***Check the box that says "Save OneDrive and SharePoint Online files automatically in Excel by default." This option only works with Office 365 and it saves your work as you do it (every few seconds)***
- ***Click Ok***

With the steps above, your work would be saved automatically every 10 minutes.

Note that for "AutoSave files by default in Excel" to work, your files must be in the latest file format (i.e., XLSX and not XLS).

11.2 Password Protection

Any computer user can attest to the presence of sensitive Excel files on their computer, and rightly so.

After all, Excel is used by millions of people around the world who work in industries ranging from finance to healthcare to education. Learning how to password-protect an Excel file is the greatest approach to ensure the security of any data you enter, whether you're making charts, converting PDFs, or just entering rows and rows of data.

Adding a password

- ***The first step that you need to do is launch Excel and load the file you wish to protect with a password.***
- ***In Step two, select "Info" from the "File" menu.***
- ***In step three, shield your spreadsheet by selecting that option. Choose Encrypt with Password from the selection that appears.***
- ***After that, in step four, Excel will ask you to enter a password. Choose a lengthy and obscure password, and store it securely in a password manager.***

If you forget it, you won't be able to open the Excel file again without a lot of work, so be sure you don't lose it or don't lose access to a copy of it in a safe place. To avoid losing access to sensitive information because of a forgotten password, it is recommended that you use a password manager or other comparable solution to store your passwords.

Excel will now always ask for your password whenever you try to open that particular file. It's important to remember that the password you just created will only secure this one Excel file and not all of the others on your computer. If you want the same level of security for all of your Excel files, you'll need to either password-protect each one separately or investigate more sophisticated security options.

To determine if an Excel file is protected with a password, go to the Info tab and check the Protect Workbook section. If a password is needed to access it, it will indicate as much.

11.3 Additional Security Options

If further security measures are required for your Excel file, you can apply these as well. Understanding the function of these alternate choices is crucial for developing adequate protections for your undertaking. Several other options that may come in handy are grouped under the Protect Document menu.

- *Mark as Final: This will indicate the file is complete and locked from further edits. However, this choice does not provide any security because a password cannot be used to protect the data.*

- *To prevent unauthorized modifications to the active worksheet, click the "Protect Current Sheet" button. This is a helpful feature if you only need to restrict access to a single page inside the worksheet but don't mind if others view the data as long as they don't make any changes. You'll find that you can take this precaution with the help of Workbook Structure as well, which prevents anyone without the password from making any changes to the data in the entire workbook.*

- *Restricting access to Excel files is very useful for businesses. Companies are aware that all workers have access to the company network, but that some workers may not have permission to view specific files. The Restrict Access function in Excel supports the IT-created security templates that restrict access to specific users. It's useful for large groups where only a subset of participants needs access to the document's data.*

- *Incorporate a Digital Signature: With a one-of-a-kind and unrepeatable digital signature, you can ensure that only you have control over and access to your Excel files.*

- *It's important to keep Excel files safe, but it's easy to forget to do so. Password protection is just one of many safeguards available to maintain the secrecy of your data. Check out our quick primer on encryption and our guide to keeping your files hidden in Windows 10 if you're concerned about the safety of your data.*

Chapter 12: Pivot Table

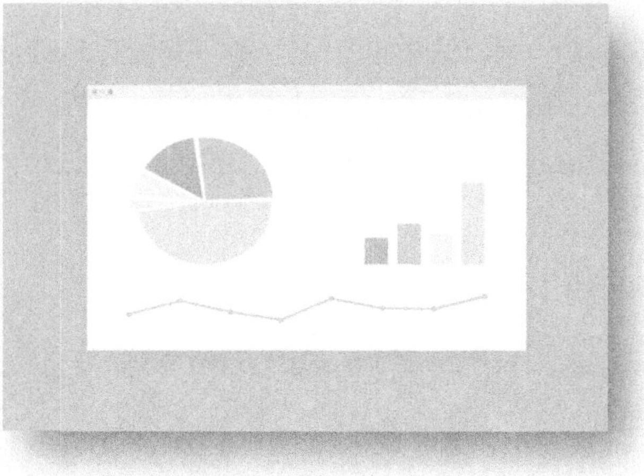

If you're looking for a simpler and more effective way to manage data for your organization, business, or any other activity that requires sorting and analyzing data, you might want to try a database. You might find that pivot tables are the best way to do what you want to do.

12.1 What Are Pivot Tables

A pivot table is a tool for summing up data that is used in a lot of business software. It is used to gather the summary of a certain set of data in a compact way. It is a very helpful tool for putting together a lot of information in Microsoft Excel. They make it easier for the user to organize data and draw conclusions from it. Rows, columns, pages, and data fields are all parts of a pivot table.

These can be moved around, and they help expand, separate, summarize, and group-specific information. All of these things can be done in real-time.

A Pivot table also refers to a programming tool that lets rows or columns of data or information be combined or rearranged. It lets anyone see the differences between a large set of data, like what you might find in a database table or a spreadsheet. Because of this, users can get data or information from the report or file without having to change it. A pivot table is a tool that will change how leaders and/or employees of a business or organization sort and analyze data from the past.

12.2 Advantages of Using Pivot Tables

- ***User-friendly***

One of the best things about pivot tables is how easy they are to

use. Everyone can easily summarize the information they have gathered. You just have to move the columns to different parts of the table. With the click of a button, users can also change the order of the columns and move them to different places.

- ***Can create instant data***

A pivot table can also make data quickly, which is another important feature. Whether the user types equations right into the pivot table or uses formulas, this tool can be used to get instant or immediate data. And this tool makes it easy for a user to compare information in a matter of seconds. It's as easy as making columns in tables where the information to compare can be dragged and dropped. This is most helpful for people who need to use a pivot table quickly.

- ***Makes data analysis easier***

Pivot tables make it much easier to analyze data. By using it, users will be able to handle and analyze a lot of data quickly and easily. With pivot tables, you can work with a lot of data in a way that only requires you to look at a small number of data fields. This will make it a lot easier to look at a lot of information.

Also, pivot tables make the process of analyzing data more interesting. It's getting more fun to do. The tables make it easy for users to drag and drop data, making the tables interactive. This is an important tool for working quickly and efficiently in Microsoft Excel.

- ***Summarizes data easily***

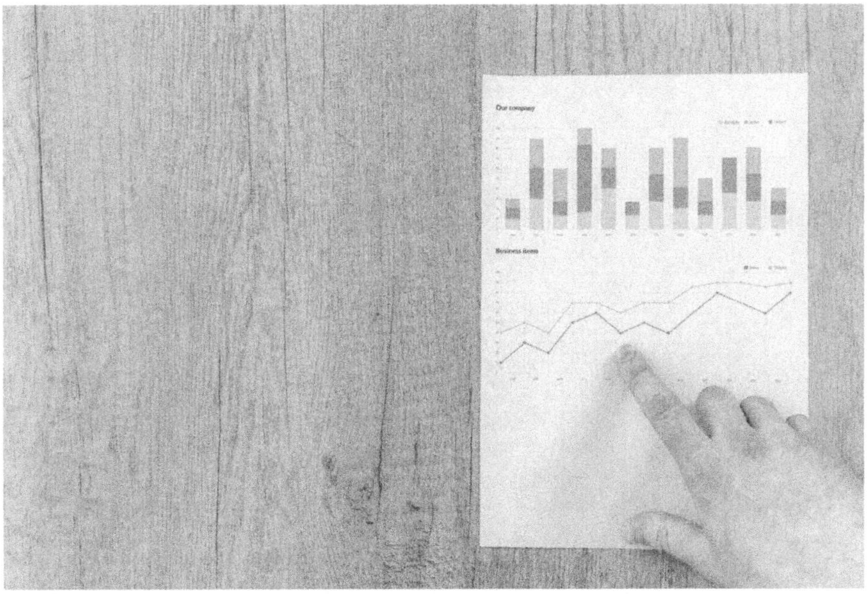

Pivot tables are a great help if you want to summarize data more quickly and easily. It will help any user make a summary from a lot of rows and columns of messy data. With this tool, you can summarize a lot of information in a small amount of space. And the data can be summed up in a very simple way that makes it easy for anyone to understand. With this tool, columns and rows can be named and arranged in any way the user wants. Data can also be set up in a way that fits their needs and how they want it to be shown. And most notably, pivot tables make it easier to divide analytical data that has been collected in a spreadsheet or database into groups.

- ***Helps to find patterns in data***

Forecasting is a very important part of running a business or any other kind of organization. In this task, Excel pivot tables can help any user make custom tables from big groups of data. And changing the data in this way will help find patterns that keep coming up in the data. In turn, this will help make accurate data forecasts.

- ***Makes it easier to make accurate reports***

Another very important thing about pivot tables is that they can help any user make presentations and reports in a very reliable and efficient way. No user will be able to make reports by hand. That will give you a lot more time to do other things and work. A user of a pivot table can also add links to external sources, if there are any, to the report they make. This makes presentations and reports more effective and convincing.

A pivot table is one of the few tools that users have access to that can help them understand analytics data better. With this tool, the same data collected in a single file can be used to make more than one report. It would stop you from using "cut and paste" and make you take more steps to get to the data a user wants. Remember that information is money in the world we live in today, and the faster you can get it, the better.

- ***Help people to decide things more quickly***

With how fast things move in the modern world, it's important to make decisions quickly. This is especially true for people in charge of a business. This can be done well with the help of a pivot table. A lot of time is saved. It is a very useful tool for reporting because it lets people look at the data and make quick decisions without much trouble. This helps a lot in the business world, where it's important to make quick, correct decisions in a short amount of time.

12.3 Example of Pivot Table

Step 1: Enter your data into columns and rows.

The pivot table in Excel begins with a basic Excel table, which is where all your data is present. To make this table, you just need to put your values in the right rows and columns. Use the top row or column to sort your values into groups based on what they mean.

Step 2: Sort your data based on a certain property.

After collecting all the required data in your Excel sheet, you would like to sort it in some way so it becomes easier to work with when you turn it into a pivot table.

To sort the data, click on the Data tab in the navigation bar at the top and then click on the Sort icon below it. In the next window, you can choose to sort the data by any column and in any order you want.

Step 3: Select the cells you want to use to make your pivot table.

Once you've sorted the data in the way you want, highlight the cells you want to summarize in a pivot table. Select the PivotTable icon by clicking the Insert button in the top menu. You can also click anywhere on your worksheet, choose "PivotTable," and manually insert the range of cells you want in the PivotTable.

This will bring up a box where you can set your cell range and choose if you want this pivot table to open in a new worksheet or stay in the one you already have. If you open a new sheet, you can use the bottom of your Excel workbook to move to and from it. When you've made your choice, click OK.

Step 4: Move a field into the "Row Labels" area by dragging and dropping it

After you finish Step 3, a blank pivot table will be created. The next step is to drag and drop a field into the Row Labels. The field should have labels that match the names of the columns of the spreadsheet. This will tell the pivot table what unique identifier (blog post title, product name, etc.) to use to sort your data.

Step 5: Move a field to the "Values" area by dragging and dropping it.

Once you've decided how you'll organize your data, drag a field into the Values area to add some values.

Step 6: Change your calculations.

By default, the sum of a value will be calculated, but you can easily change this to maximum, average, or minimum, depending on what you want to do.

You now know the basics of how to make a pivot table in Excel. With this knowledge, you can examine what you want from your pivot table and find the answers you're looking for.

For instance, you may find that the data in the pivot table isn't in the order you want. Excel's Sort feature helps you if this is the case. You might also need to add information from another source to your report, in which case the VLOOKUP function could help.

Chapter 13: Excel and Daily Life

Spreadsheet software like Microsoft Excel can store and analyze data in the form of numbers. A spreadsheet is a table that is made up of rows and columns. Letters, not numbers, are put in columns. Numbers, on the other hand, are put in rows. A place where rows and columns meet is called a "cell," and the address of a cell is a letter that stands for a row in the table of contents. Microsoft Excel may also have graphical tools, pivot tables, calculations, and basic visual programs, which is a programming language for making macros. It also has a lot of features that can help with financial, technical, and statistical problems.

Also, Excel can show data in line charts, graphs, and histograms, but it can only do a limited job of showing data in three dimensions.

- ***Keeping an eye on costs***

People usually use it to get things done because it has a lot of benefits. With the help of Microsoft Excel, it's easier to keep track of expenses. Let's say that a teacher makes around $60,000 per month. He will have to write down all of his expenses and use Microsoft Excel to figure out how much he will spend each month. You can do these things by putting information about your monthly pay and spending into Excel tables. This lets you keep track of and manage costs properly. One of the best ways to use Microsoft Excel in everyday life is to keep track of expenses.

- ***Centralizes Data into a Single Place***

Microsoft Excel's best feature is that it can put a lot of different kinds of data in one place. It helps make sure that data doesn't get lost by accident. All of the information is kept in one place. This will save you time because you won't have to look for files. You need to organize and sort data to save time when you need to get information from a file.

- ***Access to Information from the Internet***

You can use Microsoft Excel online from anywhere, which means you can use it on any device, at any time, from anywhere. It has convenient working features, which means you can do your work on your phone even if you don't have access to a computer.

Lastly, because it is very flexible, people can use it easily without having to worry about where they are or what device they are using.

- ***Security***

Since the main purpose of Microsoft Excel is to keep information safe, users can keep their information safe. Files that are saved in this program can be protected with a personal password code, which stops other people from opening or deleting them. These can be put right into the Excel spreadsheet or made with simple visual programming. Excel is also helpful because it keeps important data in a structured way and makes it easier to find than other ways of storing data. Problems can be solved quickly with the help of Microsoft Excel.

- ***It Makes the Display of data More Insightful***

Using Microsoft Excel makes it easier to show data in a way that is easier to understand. It would be better if the data bars were more useful, if certain files were highlighted, and if the data were shown in a way that was pleasing to the eye. For example, if you have data in Excel and want to draw attention to a certain part of it, you will use several parts of MS Excel's data presentation to do this. Also, spreadsheets can be made so that the data they store is more appealing to look at.

- ***Formulate what you are thinking in Mathematical Terms***

The math formulas that you can find in Microsoft Excel make your work easier. Complex math problems can be solved easily without the need for extra work from a person. You can use the program's formulas to solve problems, like figuring out the average and total of a lot of data at the same time. So, Excel is the best way to find answers and use basic math functions in tables with a lot of data.

- ***Getting data out of spreadsheets and databases***

If data is lost, Microsoft Excel makes it easy to get it back. If your important data is stored in Excel and it gets lost or damaged, you don't have to worry because the new version of Excel has a way to recover lost or damaged data.

- ***Ease the way you do your job***

Microsoft Excel has several tools that make the job easier and take less time to do. You can sort, filter, and search for data with the tool given to make your job easier. You can also use pivot tables and tables together with the tools to finish your task faster. It lets many things from big data sets be looked at with little work, and it helps find answers to questions and problems.

- ***Improvement in time management***

If you want to run a successful business or work for a large company, you'll have to do a lot of things every day. To be successful, you will need to be efficient and productive in how you run your business. In this case, Excel's many features come in handy. If you know the shortcuts that are often used in Excel, you may be able to do more work in less time and manage your time better.

Learn all of the shortcuts that are commonly used in Excel. You can also use macros and other formulas to make your computer do things for you. When you use all of Excel's subtle nudges, you can free up a lot of time to work on more difficult tasks while Excel does most of the routine, repetitive formula-based work for you.

- ***Look closely at the facts***

When working with a lot of data, it's easy to get confused. So, if you prefer to analyze data quantitatively, it will be hard for you to find big patterns and useful resources in the data you have. So, you won't be able to make good predictions based on the information you have.

In this case, Microsoft Excel could be very helpful. You can use the program's features, such as conditional formatting, to highlight rows that meet certain conditions. Having a graphic representation of all the data will save you time because you won't have to spend as much time focusing on individual data points. Instead, you'll be able to look at the whole picture and make more accurate predictions.

Excel also lets you make graphs, pie charts, histograms, and other types of graphical representations to make data easier to understand and more visually appealing. As a result of working together, everyone in your group, organization, or project will have the same understanding of the data that is being given.

Chapter 14: Excel Tips and Tricks

A spreadsheet is more than just a tab with some numbers. It's important to make your spreadsheets visually pleasing, professional-looking, and easy to understand.

No matter how many hours of research you put into your Excel presentation or how useful the information is, it won't be impressive if it looks sloppy and dull.

The secrets in this chapter can help you make a report for yourself, share information with your team, or share it with your project manager. Let's take a look at some of the most up-to-date Excel presentation tips that will help you make spreadsheets that stands out.

- ***Look for templates on the web***

If you are busy and want to get the most out of your spreadsheet without wasting time, you can choose from several templates that are made for a specific purpose and have attractive styles, fonts, and colors. To use a template, just fill in the values you want and you're ready to go.

- ***Name the worksheets clearly***
  In Excel presentations, it's mostly about being clear. For this one reason, you can't say enough about how important it is to name your project or worksheet correctly. It could be a phrase, a sentence, or even just one letter. Just make sure that you and everyone else who will be using the file can understand it.

You must also make sure that the name of the file is different from the names of other worksheets on your gadget. After all, it won't matter how many lessons you practice today if you can't find the worksheet you used them on.

- ***Define your title/header***

Your header and title can be anything, but it needs to stand out. Your file's header should tell the reader right away what the file is about.

To do this, make your header bigger, underline it, and put it in bold. Use different colors as well. Make sure that your title stands out while still fitting in with the colors and style of the template. You can also use a different font for your header.

- ***Font dos and don'ts***

Use the same font for all of your data. You can keep the same font for your header or change it. You shouldn't include more than three fonts in a single presentation if you want your worksheet to look professional.

Type of font: Always focus on how easy something is to read. For your Excel spreadsheet, sans-serif fonts are the best choice. You can use fonts like Arial, Calibri, Playfair, and Helvetica, among many others. They will help your Excel presentation look its best, especially if you use them with the right size, placement, and color of spaces.

Font size: Font 12 with is recommended to make things easier to read, but it usually depends on how they are put together.

Alignment: The alignment feature in Excel is not used very often. If you want the presentation to look professional, you should take full advantage of the alignment feature. If it's easier to line up things on the side, headers should be lined up in the middle. The text should be aligned to the left, while numbers and other numerical data should be aligned to the right. In the records input, you shouldn't put it in the middle. To wrap your title or data around a cell, click the cell, then go to the Home toolbar, click Alignment, and then wrap your text.

- ***Manage space for breathing room***

When you see a text or spreadsheet that is crowded, messy, and full of words, your brain gets tired of reading it before you even start. But if the spreadsheet is broken up into categories, it looks better and is easier for the brain to understand.

The solution is the "B2 rule," which says that you should always start your presentation on row 2 of column B and leave the first row and column blank.

Also, don't let the height and width of the document adjust them. You should be able to be flexible and creative in your workspace. Instead, change the presentation's height and width by hand so that there is just enough white space to be able to read it.

- ***Add an image***

Adding images to your spreadsheets, like a picture, a logo, or an abstract drawing, is a good way to make it better. Some of the most impressive presentations you've seen have pictures that make them look official and professional. Pictures say as much as a thousand words. Even though Excel isn't meant to look like PowerPoint, using an image can help make your presentation more memorable.

- ***Leave the grid***

Do you realize that if you erase all grid lines except the ones that went with your results, people will wonder how you did it and if you use the same version of Excel as they do? Give it a try today.

Go to the ribbon of your spreadsheet and click on the View tab. Uncheck the box next to Gridlines in the section called Show.

- ***Zebra striped***

Zebra stripes are the alternating dark and light colors in the rows, which are stacked on top of each other. This helps in a lot of different ways. First of all, it looks good and makes your work look more organized, which is especially important if you have hundreds of rows of details. Second, it makes things easier to read and connect. A reader can keep track of which row he or she is looking at by following it from the far right to the far left.

By default, when you make a table in Excel, it will look like zebra stripes. (Hint: To make a table quickly, select the data and press + T on a Mac or Ctrl + T on Windows.) On the Design page, under Table Styles, you can change the pattern and color of your zebra stripes.

It can also be done with a formula in conditional formatting, if necessary. Conditional formatting is done by putting more emphasis on rules that meet those conditions (e.g., all odd-numbered rows). You could copy it from one cell to another using the painter method on the Home toolbar.

- ***Use graphs, tables, and charts***

Presentations are not complete without some kind of visual aid. Whether it's a chart, graph, or table, you should show the raw data in a way that can be understood at a glance. Charts, graphs, and tables are important tools to have, especially if you have a large amount of data that spans several columns and rows.

- ***Create cell styles***

Excel has many cell styles that are already set up. But you can make your favorite styles yourself. If you want the visuals to look the same, this could be a better choice than using a template. After you've used your data to make a beautiful spreadsheet, you can save the style and use it in other presentations.

Just select the cells you want to save, go to the Home toolbar, click "more" at the upper end of the style gallery, and then click "new cell style." You can name the style, modify its properties, and save it in the style dialog box that pops up.

Why change something that works well and isn't broken? But you can add a little bit of variety by changing the color palette every so often.

- ***Show restraint***

Now that you know all of these tips, you are ready to start your presentation. However, don't do too much. To find the middle ground of "just enough," you have to walk a fine line between not enough and too much. Make sure the presentation is well-balanced in general.

Conclusion

Ideally, after reading this book, you'll have realized that it's a great starting point for using Excel and creating your first spreadsheets. This manual provides several ways and approaches to help you work with Excel and begin assisting others who are new to MS Excel. As you learn more about Excel, you'll find more ways to use it in your everyday life. It is better to spend time learning than to waste time on useless activities. Know what you have to do as a student and keep in mind that learning is more important than having fun.

Tasks and daily routines are a big part of life. Different people may have different plans for each day. We still have to follow it, though. We can't imagine a world without technology because it has become so important to us. We use a lot of different technologies every day to make our lives easier and better. Think about what life would be like if there were no internet or Microsoft programs like Excel. The pictures would look like they were in black and white. So, we can conclude that Microsoft Excel is important to our everyday lives.

Printed in Great Britain
by Amazon

27003229R00066